SUPERSTAR STATS

CREATED AND PRODUCED BY GEORGIAN BAY, LLC

Copyright © 2008 by Georgian Bay, LLC
All rights reserved. Published by Georgian Bay, LLC

SCHOLASTIC and associated logos are trademarks and/or
registered trademarks of Scholastic, Inc.

Georgian Bay Staff

Bruce S. Glassman, Executive Editor
Jenifer Corr Morse, Researcher
Amy Stirnkorb, Design

ISBN 10: 1-60108-997-X
ISBN 13: 978-1-60108-997-7

10 9 8 7 6 5 4 3 2
Printed in the U.S.A.

SUPERSTAR STATS

Everything COOL About Everyone Who's HOT!

By Jenifer Corr Morse

A GEORGIAN BAY BOOK

Contents

4got✗

Entertainment

Movie Actors ★ Movie Actresses ★ Movie Directors
Music ★ Theater ★ Television

sweet!

KWL.

B4?

rider

Affleck won an
Academy Award
in 1997 for his
screenplay *Good
Will Hunting*.

**Super
Stat**

Ante up for Africa

Ben Affleck

Age: 36
Born: August 15, 1972
Birthplace: Berkeley, CA
Birth Name: Benjamin Geza Affleck

Notable Achievements

⭐ Four of Affleck's blockbusters have earned more than $200 million each—*Good Will Hunting* (1997) with $226 M, *Shakespeare in Love* (1998) with $280 M, *Pearl Harbor* (2001) with $451 M, and *Armageddon* (1998) with $555 M.

⭐ Along with Matt Damon, Affleck created the production company Live Planet, which produced the Emmy-nominated documentary series *Project Greenlight*.

⭐ For his work in the 2006 movie *Hollywoodland*, Affleck won the Supporting Actor of the Year award at the Hollywood Film Festival.

⭐ Affleck's directorial debut came in 2007 with *Gone Baby Gone*, which was praised by critics and moviegoers alike.

Jessica Alba

Age: 27
Born: April 28, 1981
Birthplace: Pomona, California
Birth Name: Jessica Marie Alba

Marie's my middle name :-)

Notable Achievements

⭐ Alba has received a Teen Choice Award, a Young Artist Award, a TV Guide Award, and a Saturn Award for her role as Max in *Dark Angel*.

⭐ Alba's highest grossing films are *Fantastic Four* with a gross of $329.5 million worldwide and *Fantastic Four: Rise of the Silver Surfer* with a worldwide gross of $287.8 million.

⭐ For her work on *Fantastic Four*, Alba was nominated for a Teen Choice Award, a MTV Movie Award, and a Imagen Foundation Award.

⭐ Alba won an MTV Movie Award for her work on the movie *Sin City*.

The combined worldwide gross of Alba's 14 major movies is $1.1 billion.

Super Stat

Aguilera is one of the world's top-selling female artists with more than 14 million albums sold in the United States and 37 million sold worldwide.

Super Stat

Christina Aguilera

Age: 29
Born: December 18, 1980
Birthplace: Staten Island, NY
Birth Name: Christina Maria Aguilera

Notable Achievements

⭐ The debut album *Christina Aguilera* was released in 1999 and had three number-one singles—"Genie in a Bottle," "What a Girl Wants," and "Come On Over Baby."

⭐ Along with Pink, Lil Kim, and Mya, Aguilera did a remake of "Lady Marmalade" for the movie *Moulin Rouge,* which earned the women a Grammy for Best Pop Collaboration with Vocals.

⭐ During her nine-year career, Aguilera has been nominated for 15 Grammy Awards and won 4 of them. She has also won 1 Latin Grammy.

⭐ In 2000, Aguilera released *Mi Reflejo,* a Spanish version of her English hits. It has sold more than 3 million copies worldwide and earned her the World Music Award for the best selling Latin artist that year.

13

The total worldwide gross of Aniston's 15 major movies $1.25 billion.

Super Stat

Jennifer Aniston

Age: 40
Born: February 11, 1969
Birthplace: Sherman Oaks, California
Birth Name: Jennifer Joanna Aniston

Notable Achievements

⭐ Aniston became one of the highest-paid TV actresses in history when she earned $1 million per episode for her role as Rachel Green during the last two seasons of *Friends*.

⭐ Aniston received five Emmy Award nominations for her work on *Friends*, winning once for Outstanding Lead Actress in a Comedy Series.

⭐ Aniston's most successful film was *Bruce Almighty* in 2003, which grossed $485 million worldwide.

⭐ Aniston has won five People's Choice Awards, five Teen Choice Awards, one Screen Actors Guild Award, and one Golden Globe Award.

The Beatles

Members: George Harrison, John Lennon, Paul McCartney, Ringo Starr
Formed: 1962
Breakup: 1970
Hometown: Liverpool, England

Notable Achievements

⭐ The Beatles have 45 gold albums, 39 platinum albums, and 24 multi-platinum albums.

⭐ Their song, "Yesterday," is the most recorded song in history with 2,500 different singers recording their own versions.

⭐ The Beatles also hold the record for the group with the most number-one singles in the United States with 20.

⭐ In 2000, a compilation album of all the Beatles' number one songs was released and sold 3.6 million copies in the first week—about 3 copies per second.

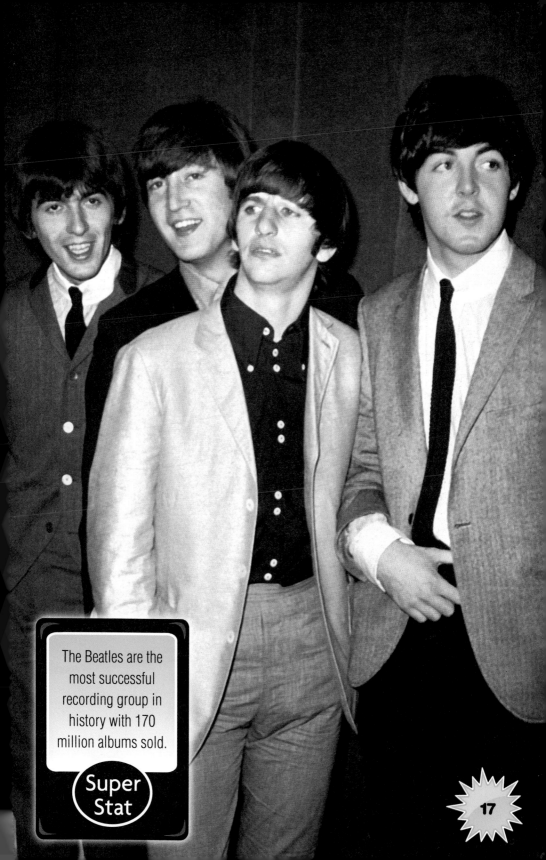

The Beatles are the most successful recording group in history with 170 million albums sold.

Super Stat

17

Bloom has starred
in 14 major movies
since 1998 with a
combined worldwide
gross of $6.5 billion!

Super
Stat

18

Orlando Bloom

Age: 32
Born: January 13, 1977
Birthplace: Canterbury, Kent, England
Birth Name: Orlando Jonathan Blanchard Bloom

Notable Achievements

⭐ Bloom's most financially successful movie is *The Lord of the Rings: The Return of the King* (2003) with a worldwide gross of $1.13 billion.

⭐ Bloom won a Screen Actors Guild Award for his role as Legolas in *The Lord of the Rings: The Return of the King* in 2003.

⭐ Bloom has starred in four of the top ten grossing films in the world—*The Lord of the Rings:The Return of the King*, *Pirates of the Caribbean: Dead Man's Chest*, *Pirates of the Caribbean: At World's End*, and *The Lord of the Rings: The Two Towers*.

⭐ Bloom has won an Empire Award (2002), two MTV Movie Awards (2002 & 2004), a Critic's Choice Award (2004), and three Teen Choice Awards (2004-2006).

John Bon Jovi

Age: 47
Born: March 2, 1962
Birthplace: Perth Amboy, NJ
Birth Name: John Francis Bongiovi

Notable Achievements

⭐ Bon Jovi is one of the top twenty best-selling bands with 34 million albums sold in the United States, and 120 million worldwide.

⭐ Bon Jovi has 13 gold albums, 11 platinum albums, and 7 multi-platinum albums.

⭐ With "Who Says You Can't Go Home"—Bon Jovi became the first rock band to reach number one on the Hot County Songs charts.

⭐ During the band's career, they've scored 19 singles on the top 40 charts, and four of them have reached number one— "I'll Be There For You," "Bad Medicine," "Livin' on a Prayer," and "You Give Love a Bad Name."

Bon Jovi holds the record
for the most weeks at
number one for a hard
rock album on the 1996
Billboard 200 chart with
"Slippery When Wet."

Super
Stat

Brooks is the best-selling male recording artist in history with a 128 million albums sold.

Super Stat

Garth Brooks

Age: 47
Born: February 7, 1962
Birthplace: Tulsa, OK
Birth Name: Troyal Garth Brooks

Notable Achievements

⭐ Brooks has 16 gold albums, 16 platinum albums, and 15 multi-platinum albums.

⭐ Brooks' "Ropin' the Wind" became the first country music album to debut on the top of the pop charts.

⭐ Brooks had one of the most successful tours in history between 1996 and 1999 when he played 350 venues and sold more than 5.3 million tickets.

⭐ Brooks' second album, *No Fences*, spent 23 weeks at number one on the Billboard Country Music chart and sold 16 million copies worldwide.

James Cameron

Age: 55
Born: August 16, 1954
Birthplace: Kapuskasing, Ontario, Canada
Birth Name: James Francis Cameron

Notable Achievements

★ Cameron has written and directed some of Hollywood's most well-known movies including *The Terminator, Terminator 2, Aliens, Titanic,* and *True Lies.*

★ Cameron received 3 of the 11 Academy Awards given to *Titanic*— Best Director, Best Picture, and Film Editing.

★ Cameron won a Golden Globe for Best Director for *Titanic.*

★ In June 2008, Cameron was inducted into Canada's Walk of Fame.

Cameron wrote and directed the blockbuster *Titanic*, which grossed more than $1.8 billion worldwide and won 11 Academy Awards.

Super Stat

Carey is the third best-selling female recording artist in the United States with 61.5 million copies sold.

Super Stat

Mariah Carey

Age: 40
Born: March 27, 1969
Birthplace: Long Island, New York
Birth Name: Mariah Angela Carey

Nick Cannon

Notable Achievements

⭐ Carey is the first recording artist in music history to have her first five singles top the Billboard Hot 100 chart.

⭐ During the World Music Awards in 2000, Carey was named the best-selling female pop artist of the millennium.

⭐ Carey has the most number-one singles by a solo artist in the United States with 18.

⭐ Carey has been nominated for 33 Grammy Awards, and won 5 of them—Best New Artist and Best Female Pop Vocal Performance (1991); and Best R&B Song, Best Female R&B Vocal Performance, and Best Contemporary R& B Album (2006).

Jackie Chan

Age: 55
Born: April 7, 1954
Birthplace: Hong Kong
Birth Name: Chan Kong-sang

Notable Achievements

⭐ Chan has received stars on the Hollywood Walk of Fame and the Hong Kong Avenue of the Stars.

⭐ In addition to acting in movies, Chan is also a producer, choreographer, and director.

⭐ Chan is a singing star in Asia and has released 20 albums. He usually sings the theme songs for his movies.

⭐ Chan does almost all of his own stunts in his films, and the Jackie Chan Stunt Team helps him coordinate them.

FITNE

Chan's combined worldwide gross of his 23 major movies totals more than $1.74 billion. His most successful movie is *Rush Hour II*.

Super Stat

On May 25, 2008, Cook made Billboard history as a solo artist by having all 11 of his singles debut on the Hot 100 at the same time.

Super Stat

David Cook

Age: 27
Born: December 20, 1982
Birthplace: Houston, TX
Birth Name: David Roland Cook

Sry bout UR Bro!

May Cook rest in peace RIP!!

Notable Achievements

⭐ Cook set another record in May 2008 by having 14 debut songs place on Billboard's Hot Digital Songs chart with downloads of more than 800,000 in one week.

⭐ Cook, who won *American Idol* 7 with 56% of the vote, sang "The Time of My Life" during the finale. The song was later released and debuted at number 3 on the Hot 100.

⭐ Before hitting it big, Cook created the song "Hold" with his band Axium. It was purchased by AMC Theatres and played before the movie previews in theaters throughout the country.

⭐ Cook's *American Idol* performance of "Billie Jean" has gotten more than 4.5 million hits on YouTube.

Miley Cyrus

Age: 17
Born: November 23, 1992
Birthplace: Franklin, Tennessee
Birth Name: Destiny Hope Cyrus

Watch the mustache

Notable Achievements

⭐ Cyrus's first single, "See You Again," reached number 10 on the Billboard Hot 100 chart, and number 6 on the Billboard Pop 100 chart.

⭐ In December 2007, *Forbes* Magazine ranked Cyrus as one on the Top 20 Earners Under 25 with her salary of $3.5 million.

⭐ Cyrus has won two Teen Choice Awards and three Kids' Choice Awards between 2007 and 2008.

⭐ In 2007, Cyrus donated one dollar for every Hannah Montana ticket sold to City of Hope—a cancer research center that helps kids.

Entertainment

The *Best of Both Worlds Concert Tour* film grossed $31.1 million during its opening weekend—more than any other movie that opened on less than 1,000 screens.

Super Stat

Matt Damon

Age: 39
Born: October 8, 1970
Birthplace: Boston, Massachusetts
Birth Name: Matthew Paige Damon

Notable Achievements

⭐ Damon's highest grossing films to date are *Saving Private Ryan* (1998) with a worldwide gross of $481.6 million, and *Ocean's Eleven* (2001) with a worldwide gross of $450.7 million.

⭐ In 1997, Damon was nominated for two Academy Awards for the movie *Good Will Hunting*, and won one for Best Original Screenplay.

⭐ For every dollar Damon earns as salary, he makes $29 at the box office. Because of this, Forbes Magazine listed him as one of the industry's most bankable stars.

⭐ Damon often donates time and money to several charities, including Not On Our Watch, GreenDimes.com, and the H2O Africa Foundation.

Damon's movies have a combined worldwide gross of $4.26 billion, which makes him one of the highest-grossing actors of all time.

Super Stat

35

Johnny Depp

Age: 46
Born: June 9, 1963
Birthplace: Owensboro, Kentucky
Birth Name: John Christopher Depp II

Notable Achievements

⭐ *Pirates of the Caribbean: Dead Man's Chest* (2007) was Depp's most financially successful movie, taking in $1.06 billion worldwide.

⭐ In 2008, Depp was ranked by Forbes Magazine as the 6th most powerful celebrity in the world, with an estimated paycheck of $72 million for the year.

⭐ During his career, Depp has been nominated for three Academy Awards, and has won a Golden Globe and a Screen Actors Guild Award.

⭐ Depp received his star on the Hollywood Walk of Fame in November 1999.

Depp has made almost 40 movies, and together they have grossed $4.77 billion worldwide.

Super Stat

Duff has released four albums—all of which achieved gold status or higher—and have collectively sold more than 13 million copies worldwide.

Super Stat

Hilary Duff

pretty

Age: 22
Born: September 28, 1987
Birthplace: Houston, TX
Birth Name: Hilary Erhard Duff

what up wl the nails

Notable Achievements

⭐ Duff's TV show *Lizzie McGuire* was a big hit on the Disney Channel, drawing more than 2.3 million viewers per show.

⭐ Duff's 10 movies—including *Agent Cody Banks, Cheaper By the Dozen*, and *A Cinderella Story*—have grossed more than $556 million.

⭐ Duff's third album, *Hilary Duff*, debuted at number two on the Billboard charts in 2004 and sold more than 1.5 million copies in less than a year.

⭐ Duff has several successful business ventures—her clothing line, "Stuff by Hilary Duff," two perfumes sold by Elizabeth Arden, and a Mattel doll in her likeness.

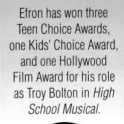

Efron has won three
Teen Choice Awards,
one Kids' Choice Award,
and one Hollywood
Film Award for his role
as Troy Bolton in *High
School Musical*.

Super
Stat

Zac Efron

Age: 22
Born: October 18, 1987
Birthplace: San Luis Obispo, California
Birth Name: Zachary David Alexander Efron

Notable Achievements

⭐ In February 2006, Efron debuted two songs on the Billboard Hot 100—"Get'cha Head in the Game" and "Breaking Free," a duet with Vanessa Hudgens.

⭐ "Breaking Free" became the fastest-climbing single at the time of release—climbing from number 86 to number 4 in two weeks on the Billboard charts.

⭐ In August 2007, *High School Musical 2* became the most-watched basic cable program in history with more than 17 million viewers.

⭐ Efron won a Young Hollywood Award for his role as Link Larkin in *Hairspray* in 2007.

Dakota Fanning

Age: 15
Born: February 23, 1994
Birthplace: Conyers, GA
Birth Name: Hannah Dakota Fanning

Notable Achievements

⭐ Fanning is the youngest person ever to be invited to join the Academy of Motion Picture Arts and Sciences.

⭐ For her work on *The War of the Worlds*, Fanning won a Saturn Award, a BFCA Award, and a Sierra Award.

⭐ Between 2004 and 2005, Fanning had starring roles in six major movies—*Nine Lives*, *Man on Fire*, *Hide and Seek*, *Dreamer: Inspired by a True Story*, *War of the Worlds*, and *Charlotte's Web*.

⭐ Even though she's young, Fanning is already bringing in the big bucks—she earns between $3 to $4 million a movie.

UPU

PU

At the age of 8, Fanning became the youngest person to be nominated for a Screen Actors Guild Award, for her supporting performance in *I Am Sam* (2001).

Super Stat

In 2007, Fergie won an American Music Award for Favorite Female Artist.

Super Stat

Fergie

Age: 34
Born: March 27, 1975
Birthplace: Hacienda Heights, CA
Birth Name: Stacy Ann Ferguson

Notable Achievements

⭐ Fergie's debut album—*The Dutchess*—launched six chart hits, including "London Bridge," "Fergalicious," "Glamorous," "Big Girls Don't Cry," "Clumsy," and "Finally."

⭐ Fergie was nominated for a Grammy Award for her song "Big Girls Don't Cry."

⭐ Fergie won three MTV Video Music Awards for her songs "Fergalicious" and "Big Girls Don't Cry" between 2007 and 2008.

⭐ *The Dutchess* is one of just seven albums by a female artist to have five or more Top Five chart hits.

America Ferrera

Age: 24
Born: April 18, 1984
Birthplace: Los Angeles, CA
Birth Name: America Georgina Ferrera

Notable Achievements

⭐ During just two seasons of her comedy *Ugly Betty*, Ferrera has won an Emmy, a Golden Globe, a Screen Actors Guild, and a Family Television award for her portrayal of Betty Suarez.

⭐ Ferrera's two major films—*Lords of Dogtown* and *The Sisterhood of the Traveling Pants*—both opened in the United States on Friday, June 3, 2005.

⭐ With her film debut of *Real Women Have Curves*, Ferrera won the Sundance Film Festival's Best Actress award in 2002.

⭐ Ferrera was her high school's valedictorian and went on to study International Relations and Theater at the University of Southern California.

Lloyds of London has insured Ferrera's smile for $10 million.

Super Stat

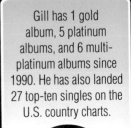

Gill has 1 gold album, 5 platinum albums, and 6 multi-platinum albums since 1990. He has also landed 27 top-ten singles on the U.S. country charts.

Super Stat

Vince Gill

Nice Hair LoL

Age: 52
Born: April 12, 1957
Birthplace: Oklahoma City, Oklahoma
Birth Name: Vincent Grant Gill

Notable Achievements

⭐ Gill has won 19 Grammy Awards—more than any other male country artist.

⭐ Gill has sold more than 24 million albums in the United States.

⭐ Gill has won 18 Country Music Awards since 1990, including Album of the Year, Song of the Year, and Male Vocalist of the Year.

⭐ In 2007, Gill was inducted into the Country Music Hall of Fame.

Green Day has sold more than 65 million albums worldwide, including 22 million in the United States.

Super Stat

Green Day

Members: Billie Joe Armstrong, Mike Dirnt, Tré Cool
Formed: 1987
Hometown: Oakland, CA

Notable Achievements

⭐ Green Day has won three Grammy Awards—Record of the Year for "Boulevard of Broken Dreams" (2006), Best Rock Album for *American Idiot* (2005), and Best Alternative Album for *Dookie* (1995).

⭐ In 2005, Green Day won seven MTV Music Awards—included the Viewer's Choice Award—for *American Idiot*.

⭐ At the American Music Awards in 1996, Green Day won Favorite Artist, Favorite Hard Rock Artist, and Favorite Alternative Artist for the album *Insomniac*.

⭐ The band's first album—*Dookie*—achieved diamond status, selling more than 10 million copies.

John Grisham

Age: 54
Born: February 8, 1955
Birthplace: Jonesboro, Arkansas
Birth Name: John Grisham Jr.

Scary!

Notable Achievements

⭐ Nine of Grisham's best-selling books have been turned into highly successful movies, including *The Firm* (1993), *The Pelican Brief* (1993), *A Time To Kill* (1996), and *Runaway Jury* (2003).

⭐ Before writing best-selling novels, Grisham practiced law and served in the House of Representatives from 1983 to 1990.

⭐ *The Firm* spend 47 weeks on the New York Times Best Sellers list and was the best-selling book in 1991.

⭐ Grisham has written one novel a year since 1988, and all of them have become international best sellers.

As of 2008, all of Grisham's 21 novels have collectively sold more than 225 million copies worldwide and have been translated into 29 languages.

Super Stat

Holmes has appeared in 15 major movies with a combined worldwide gross of $713 million.

Super Stat

Katie Holmes

Age: 31
Born: December 18, 1978
Birthplace: Toledo, Ohio
Birth Name: Kate Noelle Holmes

grow your hair and change the color

Notable Achievements

⭐ *Batman Begins* is Holmes' most financially successful movie, grossing $371.8 million worldwide.

⭐ Holmes won an MTV Movie Award for her role in *Disturbing Behavior* in 1999.

⭐ Holmes has been nominated for five Teen Choice Awards, two MTV Movie Awards, and two Saturn Awards.

⭐ Holmes is the only cast member of *Dawson's Creek* to appear in all 128 episodes.

Hudgens came in at number seven on the Forbes list of "Top-Earning Stars Under 21" with an estimated income of $2 million in 2007.

Super Stat

Vanessa Hudgens

Age: 21
Born: December 14, 1988
Birthplace: Salinas, California
Birth Name: Vanessa Anne Hudgens

Change Ur attitude

Notable Achievements

⭐ In 2006, Hudgens won A Teen Choice Award with her co-star Zac Efron for Choice Chemistry in *High School Musical.*

⭐ At the 2007 Teen Choice Awards, Hudgens won the award for Choice Breakout Singer for her debut album, *V.*

⭐ The *High School Musical* soundtrack, on which Hudgens is featured, became the best-selling album of 2006 with 3.72 million copies sold.

⭐ *The High School Musical* DVD became the fastest-selling TV movie of all time when it sold 1.2 million copies during its first week of release.

Peter Jackson

Age: 48
Born: October 31, 1961
Birthplace: Pukerua Bay, North Island, New Zealand
Birth Name: Peter Jackson

Notable Achievements

⭐ Jackson has been nominated for eight Academy Awards, and won three for Best Director, Best Picture, and Best Writing for *Lord of the Rings: The Return of the King* in 2004.

⭐ For *King Kong* in 2005, Jackson was paid $20 million upfront and 20% of the box office rentals—the highest salary paid to a director in advance of a production.

⭐ Jackson has been nominated for four Golden Globes, and won one for Best Director for *Lord of the Rings: The Return of the King* in 2004.

⭐ Jackson has his own production company—Wingnut Films.

Jackson directed *The Lord of The Rings* trilogy, which has a combined worldwide gross of $1.03 billion. All 3 rank in the top 15 highest-grossing movies of all time.

Super Stat

Since she first graced the silver screen in 1982, Jolie has appeared in 25 films with a combined worldwide gross of $2.44 billion.

Super Stat

Angelina Jolie

Age: 33
Born: June 4, 1975
Birthplace: Los Angeles, CA
Birth Name: Angelina Jolie Voight

Notable Achievements

⭐ Jolie's most successful movie—*Mr. & Mrs. Smith*—co-starred Brad Pitt and brought in a whopping $468.3 million worldwide.

⭐ Jolie has appeared in music videos for Meatloaf, Lenny Kravitz, Korn and the Rolling Stones.

⭐ She was appointed Goodwill Ambassador for the United Nations High Commissioner for Refugees in Geneva, Switzerland, after her visits to Sierra Leone, Tanzania and Pakistan.

⭐ Jolie donates millions of dollars each year to organizations such as Global Action for Children, Doctors Without Borders, and the Jolie/Pitt Foundation.

The brothers' second album, *Jonas Brothers*, reached number five on the Billboard Hot 200 chart when it was released in August 2007.

Super Stat

Jonas Brothers

Members: Kevin Jonas, Joe Jonas, Nick Jonas, John Taylor, Greg Garbowski, Jack Lawless
Formed: 2005
Hometown: Wyckoff, NJ

Notable Achievements

⭐ In 2007, the brothers performed on H*annah Montana, the Miss Teen USA Contest, the American Music Awards, The Macy's Thanksgiving Day Parade,* and *Dick Clark's New Years Rockin' Eve.*

⭐ The Jonas Brothers have been a part of many successful tours, including *Kelly Clarkson, Jesse McCartney,* and *The Backstreet Boys.*

⭐ The band filmed the movie *Camp Rock* for the Disney Channel, and it was seen by 17 million viewers within three days of the premiere on June 20, 2008.

⭐ Nick Jonas has appeared in several Broadway plays, including *Annie Get Your Gun, Beauty and the Beast,* and *Les Miserables.*

Alicia Keys

Age: 28
Born: January 25, 1980
Birthplace: New York, NY
Birth Name: Alicia Augello-Cook

Pretty

Notable Achievements

⭐ Keys has won 17 Billboard Music Awards, 3 American Music Awards, 14 NAACP Image Awards, and 11 Grammy Awards.

⭐ *The Diary of Alicia Keys* (2003) became the sixth biggest-selling album by a female artist and the second biggest-selling album by a female R&B artist with more than 9 million copies sold.

⭐ In 2007, Keys had the most successful week of her career when her album *As I Am* debuted at number one on the Billboard 200 chart and sold 742,000 copies.

⭐ Keys began to play the piano at age 7, and went on to write her first song at age 14.

With her debut album
Songs in A Minor in
2002, Alicia Keys is one
of only three singers to
win 5 Grammy Awards
in one year.

**Super
Stat**

Nicole Kidman

Age: 42
Born: June 20, 1967
Birthplace: Honolulu, Hawaii
Birth Name: Nicole Mary Kidman

Notable Achievements

⭐ Kidman's two most financially successful movies include *Happy Feet* (2006) with a worldwide gross of $385 million, and *His Dark Materials: The Golden Compass* with a worldwide gross of $366 million.

⭐ For her role as Virginia Wolfe in *The Hours*, Kidman won an Academy Award and became the first Australian actress to do so.

⭐ Chanel No. 5 perfume paid Kidman $3.71 million to make a three-minute commercial, making her the highest-paid actress per minute.

⭐ Kidman has won three Golden Globes, two MTV Movie Awards, and seven Prestige Academy of Motion Pictures Awards.

Kidman has made more than 33 movies since 1989, with a combined worldwide gross of $2.99 billion.

Super Stat

Through her work on albums, movies, and television commercials, Knowles earned more than $80 million in just one year.

Super Stat

Beyoncé Knowles

Age: 28
Born: September 4, 1981
Birthplace: Houston, TX
Birth Name: Beyoncé Giselle Knowles

tone it down

Notable Achievements

⭐ Beyoncé's debut album *Dangerously In Love* had two number one singles—"Crazy In Love" and "Baby Boy"—and earned her five Grammy Awards in 2004.

⭐ In 2004, Beyoncé and her mother launched their own clothing line called House of Dereon.

⭐ Beyoncé has starred in several hit films while creating songs for their soundtracks, including *Dreamgirls*, *Austin Powers Goldmember*, and *The Fighting Temptations*.

⭐ Beyoncé's group, Destiny's Child, is the best-selling female recording group of all time with 17.5 million albums sold.

Ashton Kutcher

Age: 30
Born: February 7, 1978
Birthplace: Cedar Rapids, IA
Birth Name: Christopher Ashton Kutcher

Notable Achievements

⭐ For his hit MTV show *Punk'd,* Kutcher served as co-creator, co-producer, and host.

⭐ Kutcher has won the most individual Teen Choice Awards with 12 surfboard trophies.

⭐ Before hitting it big with TV and movie roles, Kutcher modeled Calvin Klein jeans and did runway shows in Paris and Milan.

⭐ Kutcher, along with his wife Demi Moore, has donated millions of dollars to charities including Habitat for Humanity and St. Jude's Children's Hospital.

Kutcher's biggest box office success was *Cheaper By the Dozen* in 2003 which earned $190 million worldwide.

Super Stat

Heath Ledger

Born: April 4, 1979
Birthplace: Perth, Australia
Died: January 22, 2008
Birth Name: Heath Andrew Ledger

Notable Achievements

⭐ Ledger's final role was the Joker in *The Dark Knight,* which opened July 19, 2008. The movie set a record for the highest opening weekend with a gross of $155.3 million.

⭐ Ledger was an aspiring director, and started making music videos in Australia in 2006.

⭐ In 2006, Ledger started his own music label—Masses Music.

⭐ Ledger was nominated for an Academy Award and a Golden Globe for Best Actor for his role as Ennis Del Mar in *Brokeback Mountain* (2005). Although he lost, he did pick up an Australian Film Institute Award, a NYFCC Award for Best Actor, and an MTV Movie Award for his performance.

Ledger starred in 14 major films grossing more than $898.9 million worldwide.

Super Stat

The *George Lopez Show* is the second-longest running sitcom in tv history with Hispanic actors as the main stars.

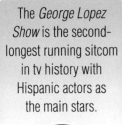

Super Stat

George Lopez

Age: 48
Born: April 23, 1961
Birthplace: Mission Hills, CA
Birth Name: George C. Lopez

Notable Achievements

⭐ In 2004, Lopez released the album *Team Leader,* which was nominated for a Grammy for Best Comedy Album.

⭐ Lopez has won several awards during his career, including a Imagen Vision Award, a Latino Spirit Award for Excellence in Television, a National Hispanic Media Coalition Impact Award, and a Spirit of Liberty Award.

⭐ Lopez founded his own charity—The George & Ann Lopez-Richie Alarcon CARE Foundation—which donates money for arts in education.

⭐ Lopez made 11 movies between 1990 and 2008, in addition to releasing 5 comedy albums between 1996 and 2007.

George Lucas

Age: 65
Born: May 14, 1944
Birthplace: Modesto, CA
Birth Name: George Walton Lucas Jr.

Notable Achievements

⭐ The combined gross of Lucas's five major movies—including four *Star Wars* blockbusters—totals $1.69 billion, with an average gross of $339.6 million.

⭐ The American Film Institute awarded a Lifetime Achievement Award to Lucas in June 2005.

⭐ Lucas created Skywalker Sound and Industrial Light & Magic—two visual and sound studios that are considered the best in the industry.

⭐ Lucas has been nominated for four Academy Awards—two for *American Graffiti* and two for *Star Wars*.

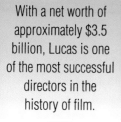

With a net worth of approximately $3.5 billion, Lucas is one of the most successful directors in the history of film.

Super Stat

Madonna's 2006
Confessions Tour
earned $260 million
and became the highest
grossing tour ever by
a female artist.

Super
Stat

Madonna

Age: 51
Born: August 16, 1958
Birthplace: Bay City, Michigan
Birth Name: Madonna Louise Veronica Ciccone

Notable Achievements

⭐ In 2008, *Forbes* Magazine ranked Madonna number 21 on the list of the world's most powerful celebrities and estimated her income for the year at $40 million.

⭐ Since her career began in 1983, Madonna has created 18 gold albums, 17 platinum albums, and 12 multi-platinum albums with total career sales of 200 million copies worldwide.

⭐ Madonna has received seven Grammy Awards and four MTV Video Awards.

⭐ In 1996, Madonna earned a Golden Globe for her title role in the movie *Evita*.

Maroon 5

Members: Adam Levine, James Valentine, Jesse Carmichael, Michael Madden, Matt Flynn

Formed: 1995

Hometown: Los Angeles, California

Notable Achievements

★ Maroon 5's debut album, *Songs About Jane,* was released in June 2002 and went triple platinum, launching the hit songs "Harder to Breathe," "She Will Be Loved," and "Sunday Morning."

★ Maroon 5's second album, *It Won't Be Soon Before Long*, debuted at number one on the Billboard 200 and went on to sell 3.5 million copies worldwide.

★ After *It Won't Be Soon Before Long* was released in May 2007, it broke iTunes sales records; 101,000 downloads in one week.

★ The single, "It Makes Me Wonder" jumped from number 64 to number 1 on the Billboard 100 chart during the first week of May 2007—the biggest jump in Billboard history.

Maroon 5 has won three Grammy Awards, two Billboard Music Awards, an MTV Video Music Award, and a World Music Award.

Super Stat

Mayer's had three albums achieve multi-platinum status—*Room for Squares*, *Heavier Things*, and *Continuum*.

Super Stat

John Mayer

Age: 32
Born: October 16, 1977
Birthplace: Bridgeport, CT
Birth Name: John Clayton Mayer

I thot. u were lead singer in Rascal Flats

Notable Achievements

⭐ Mayer won his first Grammy Award in 2003 for Best Male Pop Vocal Performance for "Your Body Is a Wonderland."

⭐ In 2007, Mayer won a Grammy for Best Pop Vocal Album for *Continuum*, and a Grammy for Best Male Pop Vocal Performance for "Waiting for the World to Change."

⭐ Mayer has won two American Music Awards (2003 & 2005), an MTV Video Music Award (2003), a People's Choice Award (2005), and a World Music Award (2005).

⭐ Mayer also donates his time to many philanthropic activities, including raising money for education and the arts, as well as raising awareness of global warming.

Brad Pitt

Age: 46
Born: December 18, 1963
Birthplace: Shawnee, OK
Birth Name: William Bradley Pitt

Notable Achievements

⭐ Pitt earned Academy Award nominations for his role in *12 Monkeys* in 1995, and for his role in *Babel* in 2006.

⭐ Pitt has won four MTV Movie Awards for his roles in *Interview With a Vampire*, *Se7en*, and *Mr. & Mrs. Smith*.

⭐ Pitt co-produced Martin Scorsese's crime-thriller *The Departed* in 2006, which won the Academy Award for Best Picture.

⭐ Pitt pledged $5 million toward building 150 new homes to help the victims of Hurricane Katrina.

The three movies in Pitt's *Ocean's Eleven* trilogy have a combined gross of more than $1.1 billion worldwide.

Super Stat

Presley is the second best-selling recording artist of all time with 118.5 million copies sold.

Super Stat

Elvis Presley

Born: January 8, 1935
Birthplace: Tupelo, Mississippi
Died: August 16, 1977
Birth Name: Elvis Aron Presley

Notable Achievements

⭐ Presley had 22 number-one singles in the United States—more than any other artist. He also had the most chart hits with 131.

⭐ "Hound Dog"/"Don't Be Cruel" is the third-most successful single of all time with 4 million copies sold.

⭐ Presley appeared in more than 30 films, which collectively earned about $150 million at the box office.

⭐ Presley has been inducted into four halls of fame—Rock and Roll Hall of Fame, Rockabilly Hall of Fame, Gospel Music Hall of Fame, and Country Music Hall of Fame.

Rihanna

Age: 21
Born: February 20, 1988
Birthplace: St. Michael, Barbados
Birth Name: Robyn Rihanna Fenty

Notable Achievements

⭐ Rihanna is the first female recording artist from Barbados to win a Grammy Award.

⭐ Rihanna's first single—"Pon de Replay" in 2005—reached number two in the Billboard Hot 100 chart in the United States.

⭐ Rihanna's first album—*Music of the Sun*—achieved gold status in the United States, and sold more than 2 million copies worldwide.

⭐ In 2007, Rihanna's hit single "Umbrella" was named the most successful song in the world for that year.

In just three years,
Rihanna has scored
11 number one singles
on the Billboard charts,
and 4 number ones
on the Hot Dance
Club Play chart.

Super
Stat

Entertainment

The Rolling Stones have made more than 65 albums since 1962, with combined total worldwide sales exceeding 200 million copies.

Super Stat

Rolling Stones

Members: Mick Jagger, Keith Richards, Charlie Watts, Ronnie Woods
Formed: 1962
Hometown: London, England

Notable Achievements

- The Rolling Stones have 42 gold albums, 28 platinum albums, and 11 multi-platinum albums.

- The Rolling Stones have sold 66 million albums in the United States—the seventh best-selling band in history.

- With a final gross of $437 million, the Stones' *Bigger Bang Tour* is the highest-grossing tour ever.

- Beginning in 1971, the Stones had eight consecutive studio albums reach number one on the U.S. Billboard charts.

JK Rowling

Age: 44
Born: July 31, 1965
Birthplace: Yate, England
Birth Name: Joanne Kathleen Rowling

Notable Achievements

⭐ Rowling has won many awards for her *Harry Potter* books, including two Booksellers Association Author of the Year Awards (1998 & 1999), a WH Smith Children's Book of the Year (2000) and in 2004, a WH Smith's Fiction Award (2004), and a British Book Award (2006).

⭐ Rowling's seventh book, *Harry Potter and The Deathly Hallows*, broke all sales records when it sold 11 million copies in 24 hours upon release in the United States and the UK on July 21, 2007.

⭐ The first four *Harry Potter* books have been made into movies, and have collectively grossed $3.7 billion worldwide.

Rowling is the mastermind behind the *Harry Potter* series, which began in 1998 and has sold almost 400 million copies worldwide.

Super Stat

For each dollar that Sandler gets paid, his movies average $9 of gross income.

Super Stat

Adam Sandler

Age: 42
Born: September 9, 1966
Birthplace: Brooklyn, NY
Birth Name: Adam Richard Sandler

Notable Achievements

⭐ Sandler's 25 movies have grossed a total of $2.20 billion worldwide. The most successful was *Click* in 2006, earning $237.6 million.

⭐ Sandler has three Emmy Award nominations and one Golden Globe nomination.

⭐ Sandler got his start in TV, including roles on the *Cosby Show*, MTV's *Remote Control*, and *Saturday Night Live*.

⭐ Sandler has a film production company called Happy Madison—a combination of two of his hit movie titles, *Happy Gilmore* (1996) and *Billy Madison* (1995).

95

Carlos Santana

Age: 62
Born: July 20, 1947
Birthplace: Autlán De Navarro, Mexico
Birth Name: Carlos Augusto Alves Santana

Notable Achievements

⭐ Santana's album *Supernatural* featured collaborations with Rob Thomas, Eric Clapton, Lauryn Hill, Dave Mathews, and many others. The album has sold more than 15 million copies and earned 9 Grammy Awards.

⭐ During his solo career, Santana has achieved 2 gold albums, 1 platinum album, and 1 diamond album.

⭐ The single "Smooth" with Rob Thomas was number 1 on the Billboard charts for 12 weeks in 1999.

⭐ As a part of the band Santana, he has 6 platinum albums and 7 gold albums.

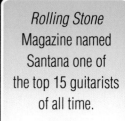

teen CHOICE '7

Seacrest has been the host of *American Idol* since it debuted in 2002. The show is continuously in the top five most-watched programs each year.

Super Stat

Ryan Seacrest

Age: 35
Born: December 24, 1974
Birthplace: Atlanta, Georgia
Birth Name: Ryan John Seacrest

Notable Achievements

⭐ Seacrest received his star on the Hollywood Walk of Fame in April 2005.

⭐ In January 2006, Seacrest signed a $21 million deal with E! to produce various shows including E! News.

⭐ Seacrest won a Daytime Emmy Award for his work on the 2005 Walt Disney World Christmas Parade.

⭐ Seacrest also hosts a Top 40 radio countdown heard on 400 stations worldwide.

Jerry Seinfeld

Age: 55
Born: April 29, 1954
Birthplace: Brooklyn, NY
Birth Name: Jerome A. Seinfeld

Notable Achievements

⭐ *TV Guide* ranked *Seinfeld* as the Greatest American Television Show of All Time in 2002.

⭐ *Seinfeld* was one of the top-two rated shows during its last five seasons between 1994 and 1998.

⭐ Seinfeld lent his voice to Barry Bee Benson in *Bee Movie*, which grossed $287 million worldwide.

⭐ Seinfeld also became a best-selling author when his book, *Seinlanguage*, made it to number one on the New York Times bestsellers list.

Seinfeld won one Emmy Award, one Golden Globe Award, two Screen Actors Guild Awards, and two American Comedy Awards for his work on his TV show *Seinfeld*.

Super Stat

Jessica Simpson

Age: 29
Born: July 10, 1980
Birthplace: Abilene, Texas
Birth Name: Jessica Ann Simpson

Notable Achievements

⭐ In 1999, Simpson's debut album *Sweet Kisses* was a double-platinum success. Its most successful single, "I Wanna Love You Forever," reached number 3 on the Billboard Hot 100 chart.

⭐ Simpson has won three Teen Choice Awards and two MTV Video Music Awards.

⭐ In 2001, Simpson's *Irresistible* broke the top 20 on four different charts—the Hot 100, the Rhythmic Top 40, the Top 40 Mainstream, and the Top 40 Tracks.

⭐ In 2005, Simpson co-starred as Daisy Duke in *The Dukes of Hazzard*, which grossed $110 million worldwide.

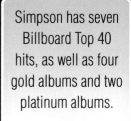

Simpson has seven Billboard Top 40 hits, as well as four gold albums and two platinum albums.

Super Stat

Will Smith

Age: 41
Born: September 25, 1968
Birthplace: Philadelphia, Pennsylvania
Birth Name: Willard Christopher Smith, Jr.

Notable Achievements

⭐ Smith has made more than 15 major movies with a combined worldwide gross of more than $5.5 billion. Smith's three highest-grossing movies are *Independence Day* (1996) with a worldwide gross of $817 million, *Men in Black* (1997) with a worldwide gross of $589 million, and *I Am Legend* (2007) with a worldwide gross of $584.

⭐ Smith's first solo album, *Big Willie Style* is certified nine times platinum and includes several huge singles—"Men in Black," "Gettin' Jiggy Wit It," and "Miami."

⭐ Smith has won three Grammy Awards, three MTV Movie Awards, three Blockbuster Awards, and one BET Award.

⭐ Smith wrote a children's book, *Just the Two of Us* in 2001, based on his hit single with the same title.

Smith became one of just two hip-hop artists to be nominated for an Academy Award when he was nominated for his work on *Ali* in 2001.

Super Stat

Steven Spielberg

Age: 63
Born: December 18, 1946
Birthplace: Cincinnati, Ohio
Birth Name: Steven Allan Spielberg

Notable Achievements

⭐ Spielberg has directed some of the most successful and well-known movies of all time, including *Jaws, ET: The Extra-Terrestrial, Indiana Jones & The Temple of Doom, Jurassic Park*, and *The War of the Worlds*.

⭐ Spielberg has won three Academy Awards—two for Best Director on *Schindler's List* (1993) and *Saving Private Ryan* (1998), and one for Best Picture on *Schindler's List*.

⭐ Spielberg was a co-founder of the highly successful production company DreamWorks, which produced box office hits such as *Shrek, Bee Movie, Kung Fu Panda*, and *Madagascar*.

⭐ In 2009, Spielberg won the Cecil B. Demille Award for Lifetime Achievement at the Golden Globes.

Spielberg has directed more than 25 major films that have a combined worldwide gross of nearly $8 billion.

Super Stat

Gwen Stefani

Age: 40
Born: October 3, 1969
Birthplace: Anaheim, CA
Birth Name: Gwen Renee Stefani

Notable Achievements

⭐ As the lead singer of No Doubt, the band's album *Tragic Kingdom* achieved diamond status with 10 million copies sold.

⭐ Stefani's third solo single—"Hollaback Girl"—is the first digital download in the United States to sell more than 1 million copies.

⭐ Stefani won the World's Best-Selling New Female Artist at the World Music Awards in 2005.

⭐ In 2004, Stefani was nominated for a Screen Actor's Guild Award for her role as Jean Harlow in *The Aviator.*

Including solo albums and collaborations, Stefani has sold more than 30 million albums worldwide.

Super Stat

Barbra Streisand

Age: 66
Born: April 24, 1942
Birthplace: Brooklyn, NY
Birth Name: Barbara Joan Streisand

Notable Achievements

⭐ *The Prince of Tides* was the first motion picture directed by its female star ever to receive a Best Director nomination from the Directors Guild of America as well as seven Academy Award nominations.

⭐ Streisand has 50 gold albums, 30 platinum albums, and 13 multi-platinum albums.

⭐ Streisand has won 2 Academy Awards—Best Original Song for *A Star is Born* in 1976, and Best Actress in 1969 for *Funny Girl*.

⭐ Streisand is one of only a few entertainers who has won an Academy Award, a Primetime Emmy Award, a Grammy Award, and a Tony Award.

Streisand is the best-selling female recording artist of all time with 71 million albums sold.

Super Stat

Kiefer Sutherland

Age: 43
Born: December 21, 1966
Birthplace: London, England
Birth Name: Kiefer William Frederick Dempsey George Rufus
Sutherland

Notable Achievements

⭐ In 2006, Sutherland signed a $40 million deal to continue playing Jack Bauer on *24* for the next three years, making him television's highest-paid actor in a drama.

⭐ Sutherland's most financially successful movie is *A Few Good Men* (1992) which earned $236.5 million worldwide.

⭐ For his work on *24*, Sutherland has received ten Emmy nominations with two wins, five Golden Globe nominations with one win, and six Screen Actors Guild nominations with two wins.

⭐ Sutherland created his own independent record label—Ironworks— to promote and develop up-and-coming bands.

Sutherland has appeared in more than 30 movies since 1983 with a combined worldwide gross of $1.2 billion.

Super Stat

In 2007, Swift won a
Breakthrough Video of
the Year Award at the
CMT Music Awards
for her debut single,
"Tim McGraw."

**Super
Stat**

Taylor Swift

Age: 20
Born: December 13, 1989
Birthplace: Reading, Pennsylvania
Birth Name: Taylor Alison Swift

Pretty

Notable Achievements

⭐ Swift's self-titled debut album contained five singles that made it into the top ten on Billboard's Hot Country Songs Chart. She is also one of the few female country artists to have five consecutive singles reach the top ten.

⭐ Swift's first album was released in late 2006 and has since achieved triple-platinum status.

⭐ Swift was named the Songwriter/Artist of the Year by the Nashville Songwriters Association International in October 2007, and she is the youngest person ever to achieve this.

⭐ In 2008, Swift won two CMT Music Awards: Female Video of the Year and Video of the Year for "Our Song."

Timbaland's fifth album—
Shock Value—has sold
more than 1 million
copies worldwide, and
has broken into the top
five position on album
charts in twelve countries.

Super
Stat

Timbaland

Age: 38
Born: March 10, 1971
Birthplace: Norfolk, Virginia
Birth Name: Timothy Mosley

Notable Achievements

⭐ Timbaland's single, "Give It To Me" with Justin Timberlake and Nelly Furtado, made it to number one on Billboard's Hot 100 chart and was nominated for a Grammy Award in 2007.

⭐ Timbaland's remix of "Apologize" was in the Billboard Hot 100 chart top ten for 25 weeks—more than any other song this decade.

⭐ In 2008, Timbaland helped produce Madonna's CD "Hard Candy," which has sold over 2 million copies worldwide in less than a year.

⭐ Timbaland produced tracks for many of today's hottest hip-hop and rap artists, including 50 Cent, Ludacris, Missy Elliot, and Jay-Z.

50 ¢

Justin Timberlake

Age: 28
Born: January 31, 1981
Birthplace: Memphis, Tennessee
Birth Name: Justin Randall Timberlake

Notable Achievements

⭐ In 2004, Timberlake received two Grammy Awards for his album *Justified*—one for Best Pop Vocal Album and one for Best Male Pop Vocal Performance.

⭐ His album *FutureSex/LoveSounds* became the biggest pre-order album on iTunes in history.

⭐ In 2008, Timberlake released a duet with Madonna entitled "4 Minutes" and it reached number one on the charts in 14 countries, making it into the top five in the United States.

⭐ As a lead singer for 'N Sync, Timberlake and his band had one of the fastest selling albums in history when they released *No Strings Attached* in 2000. It sold 2.4 million copies in one week.

Timberlake's two solo albums—*Justified* (2002) and *FutureSex/LoveSounds* (2006)— have together sold 16 million copies worldwide.

Super Stat

U2

U2 has sold more than 50.5 million albums in the United States, and 170 million albums worldwide.

Super Stat

Members: Bono, The Edge, Adam Clayton, Larry Mullen, Jr.
Formed: 1976
Hometown: Dublin, Ireland

Notable Achievements

U2 has won more Grammy Awards than any other band in history. The bands' 22 awards include wins for Best Rock Duo or Group, Album of the Year, Record of the Year, Song of the Year, and Best Rock Album.

In 1987, U2 become only the fourth rock band in history to appear on the cover of *Time* Magazine.

U2 released *All That You Leave Behind* in 2000, and it debuted at number one in 22 countries. Its hit single "Beautiful Day," won 3 Grammy Awards.

In 2005, U2 had the highest-grossing tour at $260 million. More than 3 million people attended the sold-out 90-concert tour.

Carrie Underwood

Age: 26
Born: March 10, 1983
Birthplace: Muskogee, OK
Birth Name: Carrie Marie Underwood

Notable Achievements

⭐ After winning season 4 of *American Idol*, Underwood released her debut album *Some Hearts* in 2005 and sold more than 315,000 copies during the first week of release. This is the biggest debut on the country billboard charts ever, and the album has gone on to sell more than 7 million copies.

⭐ In November 2006, Underwood won the Breakthrough Artist of the Year Award at the American Music Awards.

⭐ Underwood was inducted into Nashville's Grand Ole Opry in 2008.

⭐ During the 2007 CMT Awards, Underwood's song "Before He Cheats" won for Video of the Year, Female Video of the Year, and Video Director of the Year.

Underwood earned
two American Country
Music Awards—Best
New Female Vocalist and
Single of the Year—for
her song "Jesus, Take the
Wheel" in 2006.

Super
Stat

In 2006, West released *Late Registration*, which sold more than 850,000 copies in one week and has reached triple-platinum status.

Super Stat

Kanye West

Age: 32
Born: June 8, 1977
Birthplace: Atlanta, Georgia
Birth Name: Kanye Omari West

Notable Achievements

⭐ West received eight Grammy Award nominations for *Late Registration*, and went on to win three of them, including Best Rap Album, Best Rap Solo Performance, and Best Rap Song.

⭐ In 2007, West released the album *Graduation* and sold 957,000 copies during the first week. It later won four Grammy Awards.

⭐ West has produced hit singles for Janet Jackson, Jay-Z, and Alicia Keys.

⭐ West owns his own record label—GOOD Music.

Reese Witherspoon

Age: 33
Born: March 22, 1976
Birthplace: New Orleans, Louisiana
Birth Name: Laura Jeanne Reese Witherspoon

Notable Achievements

⭐ Witherspoon earned an Academy Award, a Golden Globe, and a Screen Actors Award for her role as June Carter Cash in *Walk the Line*.

⭐ Witherspoon owns her own production company called Type A Films.

⭐ *Sweet Home Alabama* (2002) is Witherspoon's most financially successful movie, grossing $163.4 million worldwide.

⭐ Witherspoon's two *Legally Blonde* movies made more than $267 million at the box office between 2001 and 2003.

Witherspoon has appeared in 23 major movies since her debut in *The Man in the Moon* in 1991, and the combined worldwide gross totals $1.06 billion.

Super Stat

127

Sports

Baseball ✶ Basketball ✶ Bicycling ✶ Football ✶ Golf
Hockey ✶ NASCAR ✶ Olympics ✶ Skateboarding ✶ Skating
Snowboarding ✶ Soccer ✶ Tennis ✶ X-Games

Andretti is the only driver to win the Indianapolis 500, the Daytona 500, and the Formula One World Championship.

Super Stat

MARIO ANDRETTI

Age: 69
Born: February 28, 1940
Birthplace: Montona d'Istria, Italy
Birth Name: Mario Gabriele Andretti

Notable Achievements

⭐ Andretti is one of only two drivers to ever win all four of auto racing's major competitions—Formula One, IndyCar, World Sportscar Championship, and NASCAR.

⭐ Andretti is the only person to be named United States Driver of the Year in three different decades, including 1967, 1978, and 1984.

⭐ In 1993, Andretti's final IndyCar win made him the first driver to win at least one IndyCar race in four consecutive decades.

⭐ Andretti has won 109 races on major circuits.

Agassi has won eight Grand Slam singles titles—four Australian Open titles, two US Open titles, one French Open title, and one Wimbledon title.

Super Stat

ANDRE AGASSI

Age: 39
Born: April 29, 1970
Birthplace: Las Vegas, Nevada
Birth Name: Andre Kirk Agassi

Notable Achievements

⭐ Agassi is one of five male players to win all four Grand Slam singles titles, but he is the only one to do it on three different surfaces.

⭐ Agassi has won 17 ATP Master Series tournaments—more than any other player in history.

⭐ Between 1986 and 2006, Agassi won more than $31.1 million in career earnings.

⭐ In 1996, Agassi won a gold medal at the Atlanta Olympics for the men's singles competition.

Armstrong won the Tour de France a record-breaking seven times from 1999 to 2005.

Super Stat

LANCE ARMSTRONG

Age: 38
Born: September 18, 1971
Birthplace: Plano, Texas
Birth Name: Lance Edward Gunderson

Notable Achievements

⭐ Armstrong was the Associated Press's Athlete of the Year from 2002 to 2005.

⭐ The United States Olympic Committee named Armstrong Sportsman of the Year in 1999, 2001, 2002, and 2003.

⭐ In 2002, Armstrong won a bronze medal at the Olympic Games in Sydney, Australia.

⭐ After first retiring from cycling, Armstrong took up running and has completed both the New York and Boston marathons in less than 3 hours.

RONDÉ BARBER

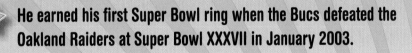

Age: 34
Born: April 7, 1975
Birthplace: Blacksburg, Virginia
Birth Name: Jamael Orondé Barber

Notable Achievements

 Barber is the Tampa Bay Buccaneer's all-time interception leader with 33 career interceptions at the end of 2007.

Barber has been selected to the Pro Bowl four times (2001, 2004-2006) and to the All-Pro five times (2001, 2002, 2004-2006).

He earned his first Super Bowl ring when the Bucs defeated the Oakland Raiders at Super Bowl XXXVII in January 2003.

Barber—a third-round draft pick in 1997—holds a team record of 11 regular-season career touchdowns by a defenseman.

Sports

In December 2005, Barber became the first cornerback in NFL history to record at least 20 sacks and 20 interceptions in his career.

Super Stat

Beckham is the first
English soccer player—
and the twenty-first
overall player—to score
in three World
Cup competitions.

Super
Stat

DAVID BECKHAM

Age: 34
Born: May 2, 1975
Birthplace: Leytonstone, London, England
Birth Name: David Robert Joseph Beckham

Notable Achievements

⭐ Beckham is the world's highest-earning soccer player, with salary, endorsements, and profit-sharing totaling $48.9 million.

⭐ Beckham earned his 100th CAP—or international appearance—for England in March 2008.

⭐ Beckham has been named FIFA Player of the Year runner-up twice (1999, 2001).

⭐ Beckham has scored 80 regular-season goals and 9 cup-goals since he started competing in 1992.

SUE BIRD

Age: 29
Born: October 16, 1980
Birthplace: Syosset, New York
Birth Name: Suzanne Brigit Bird

Notable Achievements

⭐ Bird was the first overall draft pick for the WNBA in 2002, and went on to lead her team in assists, steals, and three-point shots for the year. This was the first time in WNBA history that a point guard was the top draft pick.

⭐ In 2000 and 2001, Bird helped win the NCAA titles as a point guard for the University of Connecticut.

⭐ In 2002, Bird won the Naismith Award and was named College Player of the Year.

⭐ Bird has been named WNBA All Star four times from 2002 to 2005.

Bird won a gold medal in women's basketball at the Athens Olympics in 2004.

Super Stat

Brady helped the Patriots set a record for the longest consecutive winning streak when they won 21 games between October 2003 and October 2004.

Super Stat

TOM BRADY

Age: 32
Born: August 3, 1977
Birthplace: San Mateo, California
Birth Name: Thomas Edward Brady, Jr.

Notable Achievements

⭐ Brady has been a quarterback for the New England Patriots in four Super Bowls, winning three of them (2002, 2004, 2005). He was also named Super Bowl MVP twice (2002 and 2004).

⭐ Brady holds the record for the most passing touchdowns in a single season with 50 touchdown passes in 2007.

⭐ Brady has played in four Pro Bowls (2001, 2004, 2005, 2007).

⭐ In 2007, Brady was named AP Male Athlete of the Year, AP NFL MVP, AP NFL Offensive Player of the Year, and Sporting News Sportsman of the Year.

Brodeur is the only goalie in NHL history to win at least 40 games a season seven times in his career.

Super Stat

MARTIN BRODEUR

Age: 37
Born: May 6, 1972
Birthplace: Montreal, Quebec, Canada
Birth Name: Martin Pierre Brodeur

Notable Achievements

⭐ Brodeur—a goalie for the New Jersey Devils since his career began in 1991—has led the team to three Stanley Cup wins (1995, 2000, 2003).

⭐ Brodeur has been an NHL All Star ten times, in addition to winning the Vezina Trophy four times and the Jennings Trophy four times.

⭐ Brodeur holds many NHL records, including most overtime wins, most wins in a season, most minutes played in a season, and most combined shutouts.

⭐ At the 2002 Salt Lake City Olympics, Broduer won a gold medal for Team Canada, allowing only two goals during the entire tournament.

KOBE BRYANT

Age: 31
Born: August 23, 1978
Birthplace: Philadelphia, Pennsylvania
Birth Name: Kobe Bean Bryant

Notable Achievements

★ Bryant—a guard for the LA Lakers—is a ten-time NBA All Star, a three-time NBA Champion, a two-time All-Star MVP, a one-time NBA MVP, and a one-time NBA Slam Dunk Champion.

★ In 1996, Bryant became the only guard in NBA history to be drafted directly out of high school.

★ Bryant won a gold medal at the Beijing Olympics in 2008.

★ Bryant led the league in scoring during the 2005-2006 and 2006-2007 seasons.

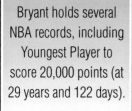

Bryant holds several NBA records, including Youngest Player to score 20,000 points (at 29 years and 122 days).

Super Stat

149

LINDSAY DAVENPORT

Age: 33
Born: June 8, 1976
Birthplace: Palos Verdes, California
Birth Name: Lindsay Ann Davenport

Notable Achievements

⭐ Davenport has won three Grand Slam singles championships—the US Open (1998), Wimbledon (1999), and the Australian Open (2000).

⭐ Davenport has also won also three Grand Slam doubles championships—the French Open (1996), the US Open (1997), and Wimbledon (1999).

⭐ At the Atlanta Summer Olympics in 1996, Davenport won a gold medal in the singles final.

⭐ Davenport has won 55 career singles titles since she turned pro in 1993.

Davenport has earned more money than any other female tennis player in history with a career total of $22.0 million since 1993.

Super Stat

DALE EARNHARDT, JR.

Age: 35
Born: October 10, 1974
Birthplace: Kannapolis, North Carolina
Birth Name: Ralph Dale Earnhardt, Jr.

Notable Achievements

⭐ In 2004, Earnhardt, Jr. won the Daytona 500.

⭐ In 2000, Earnhardt, Jr. became the first rookie to win the All Star Exhibition Race.

⭐ Earnhardt, Jr. was named NASCAR Most Popular Driver from 2003 to 2007.

⭐ Earnhardt, Jr. has his own show on XM Radio's XM Sports Nation.

MBNA
CAL RIPKEN, JR.
400
DOVER DOWNS

WINNER
September 23, 2001

MBNA

Earnhardt, Jr. has 18 NASCAR Sprint Cup Series wins and 133 top-ten finishes. In the NASCAR Nationwide Series, Earnhardt, Jr. has 22 wins and 67 top-ten finishes.

Super Stat

Favre was a
Pro Bowl selection
nine times and an
All Pro selection
seven times.

Super Stat

BRETT FAVRE

Age: 40
Born: October 10, 1969
Birthplace: Gulfport, Mississippi
Birth Name: Brett Lorenzo Favre

Notable Achievements

⭐ Favre holds many impressive NFL records, including most touchdown passes (442), most career passing yards (61,665), most career pass completions (5,377), and most career victories as a starting quarterback (160).

⭐ Favre is the only NFL Player in history to win the Associated Press MVP Award three times (1995-1997).

⭐ As quarterback, Favre led the Green Bay Packers to a Super Bowl win against the New England Patriots in 1997 at Super Bowl XXXI.

⭐ Favre was named NFC Offensive Player of the Week twelve times.

ROGER FEDERER

Age: 28
Born: August 8, 1981
Birthplace: Basel, Switzerland
Birth Name: Roger Federer

Notable Achievements

⭐ Federer was ranked the number one player in the world for a record 233 weeks.

⭐ Federer has won the Australian Open, Wimbledon, and the US Open in the same year three times.

⭐ Federer has won 56 career singles titles and 7 career doubles titles.

⭐ Federer's career earnings total more than $41.7 million since his career began in 1999.

Federer has won thirteen Grand Slam titles—three Australian Opens, five Wimbledons, and five US Opens.

Super Stat

KEVIN GARNETT

Age: 33
Born: May 19, 1976
Birthplace: Mauldin, South Carolina
Birth Name: Kevin Maurice Garnett

Notable Achievements

⭐ Garnett is a five-time regular-season leader for defensive rebounds (2003-2007), a four-time regular season-leader for rebounds per game (2004-2007), and a two-time regular-season leader for rebounds (2004-2005).

⭐ Garnett was named Most Valuable Player during the 2003-2004 season.

⭐ Garnett has played in 11 All Star Games.

⭐ Garnett won an Olympic gold medal at the Sydney Olympics in 2000.

Sports

During the 2007-2008 season, Garnett was named NBA Defensive Player of the Year.

Super Stat

Gordon has won the
Daytona 500 three times
(1997, 1999, 2005), and
the NASCAR Winston Cup
(now called the Sprint
Cup) four times (1995,
1997, 1998, 2001).

Super
Stat

JEFF GORDON

Age: 38
Born: August 4, 1971
Birthplace: Vallejo, California
Birth Name: Jeffery Michael Gordon

Notable Achievements

☆ In 1991, Gordon was named NASCAR Busch Series Rookie of the Year. In 1993, he was named Sprint Cup Rookie of the Year.

☆ Since Gordon began professional racing in 1993, he has been ranked number one four times (1995, 1997, 1998, 2001).

☆ Gordon won the Allstate 400 at the Brickyard four times—1994, 1998, 2001, and 2004.

☆ Gordon's career earnings total $95.9 million.

WAYNE GRETZKY

Age: 48
Born: January 26, 1971
Birthplace: Ontario, Canada
Birth Name: Wayne Douglas Gretzky

Notable Achievements

⭐ Gretzky is the only NHL player to score more than 200 points in one season—and he did it four times.

⭐ Gretzky was immediately inducted into the NHL Hall of Fame when he retired, bypassing the normal 3-year waiting period.

⭐ Gretzky has won three gold medals and two silver medals in the Canada Cup.

⭐ Gretzky's number 99 was retired league-wide at the 2000 NHL All Star Game.

Sports

When Gretzky retired in April 1999, he held more than 30 regular-season records, fifteen play-off records, and six All Star records.

Super Stat

163

Hamm has scored more goals than any other soccer player—male or female—in the history of MLS soccer with 158 goals.

Super Stat

MIA HAMM

Age: 37
Born: March 17, 1972
Birthplace: Selma, Alabama
Birth Name: Mariel Margaret Hamm

Notable Achievements

⭐ Hamm was named the women's FIFA World Player of the Year in 2001 and 2002.

⭐ In 2007, Hamm was inducted in to the National Soccer Hall of Fame and the Texas Sports Hall of Fame in 2008.

⭐ Hamm has won three Olympic medals—two gold medals in Athens (2004) and Atlanta (1996), and one silver in Sydney (2000).

⭐ During her career, Hamm played in 259 international games— the second most of any female soccer player.

TONY HAWK

Age: 41
Born: May 12, 1968
Birthplace: San Diego, California
Birth Name: Anthony Frank Hawk

Notable Achievements

⭐ Hawk has invented and perfected more than 40 skateboarding moves.

⭐ Hawk is the first skater to land a 900—a jump that includes two and a half rotations.

⭐ Hawk has helped to design 10 best-selling video games based on his skateboarding moves and tricks.

⭐ Six Flags has designed skateboard-themed roller coasters in four of its parks in honor of Hawk, complete with rolling and spinning board moves.

Hawk has won nine summer X-Games medals—five gold, three silver, and one bronze.

Super Stat

LeBRON JAMES

Age: 25
Born: December 30, 1984
Birthplace: Akron, Ohio
Birth Name: LeBron Raymonde James

Notable Achievements

⭐ At the age on 18, James was selected by the Cleveland Cavaliers as the first overall draft pick in 2003.

⭐ James was selected as the NBA All-Star MVP in 2006 and 2008.

⭐ James was the 2008 NBA scoring champion with 2,250 points that season.

⭐ James won a gold medal at the Olympic Games in Beijing in 2008, and a bronze medal at the Olympics in Athens in 2004.

In February 2008, James became the youngest person in NBA history to score 10,000 points at the age of 23 years and 59 days.

Super Stat

DEREK JETER

Age: 35
Born: June 26, 1974
Birthplace: Pequannock, New Jersey
Birth Name: Derek Sanderson Jeter

Notable Achievements

⭐ Since beginning his career in 1995, Jeter has won an American League Rookie of the Year Award, a Silver Slugger Award, and three Golden Glove Awards.

⭐ In 2000, Jeter became the only MLB player to win the All Star Game MPV Award and the World Series MVP Award in the same year.

⭐ Jeter has been selected to the All Star Team nine times (1998-2002, 2004, 2006-2008).

⭐ Jeter has helped the New York Yankees win the World Series four times (1996, 1998-2000).

With a ten-year contract worth more than $189 million, Jeter is one of the highest paid players in the league.

Super Stat

Johnson won four medals at the 2008 Olympic Games in Beijing—she won a gold on balance beam, and silver medals in team competition, floor exercise, and all-round.

Super
Stat

SHAWN JOHNSON

Age: 17
Born: January 19, 1992
Birthplace: Des Moines, Iowa
Birth Name: Shawn Machel Johnson

Notable Achievements

⭐ Johnson is the 2007 World All-Around Gymnastics Champion.

⭐ Johnson was the U.S All-Around Champion in 2007 and 2008.

⭐ During the Pan American Games in 2007, Johnson won four gold medals and one silver medal.

⭐ In 2006, Johnson won the junior title at the U.S. Nationals with a score higher than the senior title winner.

Jones earned a gold medal at the 2008 Olympic Games in Beijing when he and teammates Michael Phelps, Jason Lezak, and Neil Walker won the 4 X 100 freestyle relay.

Super Stat

CULLEN JONES

Age: 25
Born: February 29, 1984
Birthplace: New York, New York
Birth Name: Cullen Jones

Notable Achievements

⭐ During the 2007 World Aquatics Championships, Jones won a gold medal in the 4 X 100 meter freestyle relay and a silver medal in the 50-meter freestyle relay.

⭐ During the 2006 Pan Pacific Championships, Jones set a meet record in the 50-meter freestyle.

⭐ Jones became the first African American swimmer to hold a world record when he won the gold medal in Beijing.

⭐ In 2006, Jones was named USA Swimming Breakout Performer of the Year and Relay Performance of the Year

Sports

RED HOT & BLUE

WIZARDS
23

Jordan has been selected
as an NBA All Star
fourteen times between
1985 and 2003, and was
the game MVP in 1988,
1996, and 1998.

Super
Stat

MICHAEL JORDAN

Age: 46
Born: February 17, 1963
Birthplace: Brooklyn, NY
Birth Name: Michael Jeffrey Jordan

Notable Achievements

⭐ Jordan won the NBA Championship six times with the Chicago Bulls—1991-1993, and 1996-1998.

⭐ Jordan holds the NBA's highest career regular-season scoring average with 30.12 points per game.

⭐ Jordan has won two Olympic gold medals—one at the 1984 Olympics in Los Angeles and one at the 1992 Olympics in Barcelona.

⭐ Jordan won the NBA's Slam Dunk contest in 1987 and 1988.

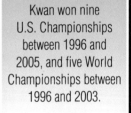

Kwan won nine
U.S. Championships
between 1996 and
2005, and five World
Championships between
1996 and 2003.

Super Stat

MICHELLE KWAN

Age: 29
Born: July 7, 1980
Birthplace: Torrance, California
Birth Name: Michelle Wingshan Kwan

Notable Achievements

⭐ Kwan won a silver medal at the 1998 Nagano Olympics and a bronze medal at the 2002 Salt Lake City Olympics.

⭐ Kwan has received a perfect score (6.0) at the national and world competitions a total of 57 times.

⭐ In 2003, Kwan was awarded the United States' Olympic Committee's (USOC) "Sportswoman of the Year." Only five other skaters have received this honor.

⭐ Kwan has been named the USOC "Athlete of the Month" fourteen times—more than any other athlete in history.

LISA LESLIE

Age: 37
Born: July 7, 1972
Birthplace: Gardena, California
Birth Name: Lisa Leslie

Notable Achievements

⭐ On July 30, 2002, Leslie became the first player to score a slam dunk in the WNBA.

⭐ Leslie was the first player in the WNBA to score 3,000 points.

⭐ Leslie won the WNBA Championship with the Los Angeles Sparks in 2001 and 2002.

⭐ Leslie has won an Olympic gold medal at the games in Atlanta (1996), Sydney (2000), and Athens (2004).

In 2001, Leslie was the
first player in the league
to earn the Regular
Season Championship,
and All Star MVP Awards
in the same season.

Super
Stat

Lilly is the most capped
player—from both the
men's and women's
soccer leagues—with
340 international
games played.

Super
Stat

KRISTINE LILLY

Age: 37
Born: July 22, 1972
Birthplace: Wilton, Connecticut
Birth Name: Kristine Marie Lilly

Notable Achievements

⭐ Lilly was named U.S. Soccer Female Athlete of the Year in 1993 and 2005.

⭐ In 2004, Lilly became the fifth player in world history to score 100 international goals.

⭐ Lilly was named FIFA Women's World Player of the Year.

⭐ Lilly has won three Olympic medals—a gold in Atlanta (1996) and Athens (2004), and a silver in Sydney (2000).

ELI MANNING

Age: 28
Born: January 3, 1981
Birthplace: New Orleans, Louisiana
Birth Name: Elisha Nelson Manning

Notable Achievements

⭐ Manning was the first-round overall draft pick in 2004. He was selected by the San Diego Chargers, but then traded later that day to the NY Giants.

⭐ In 2003, Manning won the Johnny Unitas Golden Arm Award, the Maxwell Award, and the Conerly Trophy while playing for the University of Mississippi.

⭐ Manning has completed 11,385 passing yards and 77 touchdowns in his four seasons in the NFL.

⭐ Manning has started 55 consecutive games for the Giants—the third-longest streak among active quarterbacks.

As the NY Giants starting quarterback, Manning was named the MVP of Super Bowl XLII on February 3, 2008 when they defeated the New England Patriots.

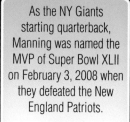

Super Stat

Manning is the first quarterback in NFL history to throw for more than 3,000 yards in the first ten seasons of his career.

Super
Stat

PEYTON MANNING

Age: 33
Born: March 24, 1976
Birthplace: New Orleans, Louisiana
Birth Name: Peyton Williams Manning

Notable Achievements

⭐ Manning has the second-highest quarterback rating of all time in the NFL with 94.7.

⭐ Manning was the MVP of Super Bowl XLI in 2006 when he led the Indianapolis Colts to victory over the Chicago Bears.

⭐ Manning has been selected to the Pro Bowl eight times (1999-2000, 2002-2007).

⭐ Manning started 160 consecutive games—the longest streak among active NFL quarterbacks.

Sports

McNabb has averaged one interception per every 46 pass attempts— the second-lowest in the NFL.

Super Stat

DONOVAN McNABB

Age: 33
Born: November 25, 1976
Birthplace: Chicago, Illinois
Birth Name: Donovan Jamal McNabb

Notable Achievements

⭐ McNabb has been selected to the Pro Bowl five times (2000-2004).

⭐ In 2004, McNabb was named NFC Offensive Player of the Year.

⭐ In 2000, McNabb was named NFL Player of the Year by CBS Radio, and was named to the All-Madden Team.

⭐ During his college career at Syracuse, McNabb was named the Big East Conference's Offensive Player of the Decade for the 1990s.

MARK MESSIER

Age: 48
Born: January 18, 1961
Birthplace: Edmonton, Canada
Birth Name: Mark John Douglas Messier

Notable Achievements

⭐ Messier is the only professional athlete to serve as captain for two different teams during his career and lead them both to championship victories. He did so with the Edmonton Oilers in 1990 and the New York Rangers in 1994.

⭐ Messier ranks second on the career lists for regular season points scored (1,887), playoff points (295), and regular season games played (1,756).

⭐ Messier played in 15 NHL All Star Games between 1982 and 2004.

⭐ In 2007, Messier was inducted into the Hockey Hall of Fame.

Messier won
six Stanley Cup
Championships
during his career.

Super
Stat

Mickelson has won three major golf championships—the Masters in 2004 and 2006, and the PGA Championship in 2005.

Super Stat

PHIL MICKELSON

Age: 39
Born: June 16, 1970
Birthplace: San Diego, California
Birth Name: Philip Alfred Mickelson

Notable Achievements

⭐ Mickelson has won 41 professional tournaments since 1991. Of those victories, 37 of them have been on the PGA Tour.

⭐ Mickelson is only the third golfer with a left-handed swing to win a major PGA tournament.

⭐ Mickelson has spent more than 500 weeks as a top ten player on the Official World Golf Ranking.

⭐ Mickelson has earned more than $49.3 million in career winnings.

YAO MING

Age: 29
Born: September 12, 1980
Birthplace: Shanghai, China
Birth Name: Yao Ming

Notable Achievements

⭐ Ming has been named to the NBA All Star team six times (2003-2008).

⭐ Ming has been selected to the All NBA Team four times (2004, 2006-2008).

⭐ The 7-foot, six-inch center is ranked 7th in the NBA in blocks per game.

⭐ *Forbes* Magazine has named Ming as China's top-earning celebrity for the last five years. Ming earned about $54 million in 2007.

In 2002, Ming was the first overall draft pick and was chosen by the Houston Rockets. He became the first international player to be selected first overall.

Super Stat

DAVE MIRRA

Age: 35
Born: April 4, 1974
Birthplace: Chittenango, New York
Birth Name: David Michael Mirra

Notable Achievements

⭐ Mirra has medaled in every X-Games since they began in 1995.

⭐ Mirra is the first BMX rider to ever pull a double backflip in competition.

⭐ In 2000, Mirra won the ESPN Action Sports and Music Award for BMX Rider of the Year.

⭐ In 2005, Mirra was named Extreme Male Athlete of the Year at the Teen Choice Awards, and Freestyler of the Year by BMX Plus.

Mirra has won more X-Games medals than any other athlete with a total of 22. He has 14 gold medals, 4 silver, and 4 bronze.

Super Stat

RAFAEL NADAL

Age: 23
Born: June 3, 1986
Birthplace: Manacor, Majorca
Birth Name: Rafael Nadal Parera

Notable Achievements

☆ Nadal won an Olympic gold medal at the 2008 Games in Beijing.

☆ In 2008, Nadal had a career-best 32-match-long winning streak.

☆ Nadal is one of only two tennis players to win four consecutive French Opens.

☆ Nadal has earned more than $19.9 million in career prize money.

Nadal has won
five Grand Slam
singles titles—the
French Open from
2005 to 2008 and
Wimbledon in 2008.

Super
Stat

STEVE NASH

Age: 35
Born: February 7, 1974
Birthplace: Johannesburg, South Africa
Birth Name: Stephen John Nash

Notable Achievements

☆ Nash led the NBA in assists per game and total assists from 2005 to 2007. He also led the league in free-throw percentages in 2006. And from 2004 to 2008, Nash led the NBA in assists per 48 minutes.

☆ In 2005 and 2006, Nash was voted NBA MVP while playing for the Phoenix Suns.

☆ Nash has also made the All NBA selection six times (2002, 2003, 2005-2008).

☆ In 2006, ESPN named Nash as the ninth-greatest point guard of all time.

Nash has been voted to six NBA All Star Games (2002, 2003, 2005-2008).

Super Stat

SHAQUILLE O'NEAL

Age: 37
Born: March 6, 1972
Birthplace: Newark, New Jersey
Birth Name: Shaquille Rashaun O'Neal

Notable Achievements

 O'Neal's career scoring average is 25.6 points per game—the ninth-highest in league history.

 O'Neal is a 13-time All-NBA First Team selection and a 14-time All Star Game selection.

O'Neal was named NBA MVP in 2000, one vote shy of a unanimous selection.

In 1996, O'Neal won an Olympic gold medal at the games in Atlanta.

O'Neal has won four
NBA Championships—
three with the Los Angeles
Lakers (2000-2002) and
one with the Miami
Heat (2006).

Super
Stat

Sports

204

Patrick's 2008 Indy Japan 300 win made her the first woman to win a major open-wheel closed course race.

Super Stat

DANICA PATRICK

Age: 27
Born: March 25, 1982
Birthplace: Beloit, Wisconsin
Birth Name: Danica Patrick

Notable Achievements

☆ In 2005, Patrick was named Rookie of the Year for both the Indianapolis 500 and IndyCar seasons.

☆ From 2005 to 2007, Patrick was voted the IndyCar Most Popular Driver.

☆ Patrick became the first female driver to lead the Indianapolis 500 when she led the pack twice during the 2005 race.

☆ Patrick scored the highest Indy 500 finish of any female driver when she came in fourth in 2005.

CARLY PATTERSON

Age: 21
Born: February 4, 1988
Birthplace: Baton Rouge, Louisiana
Birth Name: Carly Rae Patterson

Notable Achievements

⭐ Patterson won a silver medal during team competition at the Athens Olympics.

⭐ In 2002, Patterson was named the U.S. Junior National All-Around champion.

⭐ At the World Gymnastics Championship in 2003, Patterson won the all-around silver medal.

⭐ Patterson won the exclusive American Cup competition in 2003 and 2004.

Patterson won an individual all-around gold medal at the 2004 Olympic Games in Athens. She is only the second American woman to accomplish this.

Super Stat

MICHAEL PHELPS

Age: 24
Born: June 30, 1985
Birthplace: Baltimore, Maryland
Birth Name: Michael Fred Phelps

Notable Achievements

☆ Phelps won eight gold medals at the 2008 Olympic Games in Beijing, China—the highest total golds won in a single Olympics.

☆ Phelps set seven world records and one Olympic record at the Beijing Olympics.

☆ Phelps was named World Swimmer of the Year in 2003, 2004, 2006, and 2007. He was named American Swimmer of the Year in 2001, 2002, 2003, 2004, 2006, and 2007.

☆ Phelps won two bronze medals in the 2004 Olympics in Athens— one for the 200 meter freestyle and one for the 4 X 100 meter relay.

Phelps has won
14 Olympic gold
medals—more than
any other athlete in
history of the Games.

Super
Stat

ALEX RODRIGUEZ

Age: 34
Born: July 27, 1975
Birthplace: New York City, NY
Birth Name: Alexander Emmanuel Rodriguez

Notable Achievements

⭐ Rodriguez is the youngest player in MLB history to hit 500 home runs.

⭐ Rodriguez played in the All Star game twelve times between 1996 to 2008—seven times as a shortstop and five times as a third-baseman.

⭐ Rodriguez won nine Silver Slugger Awards between 1996 and 2007.

⭐ Rodriguez won the American League MVP in 2003, 2005, and 2007.

In December 2007, Rodriguez signed a 10-year contract with the Yankees worth $275 million—the most expensive contract in baseball.

Super Stat

unicef

Ronaldinho was named FIFA World Player of the Year and World Soccer Player of the Year in 2004 and 2005.

Super Stat

10

RONALDINHO

Age: 29
Born: March 21, 1980
Birthplace: Porto Alegre, Brazil
Birth Name: Ronaldo de Assis Moreira

Notable Achievements

⭐ Ronaldinho played in the FIFPro World XI in 2005, 2006, and 2007.

⭐ In 2005, Ronaldinho was named European Footballer of the Year and UEFA Club Footballer of the Year.

⭐ While playing with the National Team, Ronaldinho has played in more than 80 games and scored more than 33 goals.

⭐ Ronaldinho was the FIFA Confederations Cup Top Scorer in 1999.

During his career, Ryan struck out 5,714 batters—more than any other pitcher in history.

Super Stat

NOLAN RYAN

Age: 62
Born: January 31, 1947
Birthplace: Refugio, Texas
Birth Name: Lynn Nolan Ryan, Jr.

Notable Achievements

⭐ Ryan was inducted into the Baseball Hall of Fame in 1999 with 98.2% of the vote.

⭐ Ryan played for a record 27 seasons from 1966 to 1993.

⭐ Ryan was an All-Star selection eight times between 1972 and 1989.

⭐ Ryan holds the MLB record for the most no-hitters with seven.

OMEGA

Shell

Rosbacher

Deutsche

Schumacher has won seven Formula One Championships — 1994, 1995, 2000-2004.

Super Stat

MICHAEL SCHUMACHER

Age: 40
Born: January 3, 1969
Birthplace: Hurth-Hermulheim, Germany
Birth Name: Michael Schumacher

Notable Achievements

 Between 1991-2006, Schumacher won 91 Formula One races and had 154 podium finishes.

 In 2006, Schumacher was awarded the FIA Gold Medal for Motor Sport.

 Schumacher won Laureus World Sportsman of the Year in 2002 and 2004.

 In 2004, Schumacher set records for most wins in a season (13), fastest laps in a season (10), and points scored in a season (148). These records still stand.

MARIA SHARAPOVA

Age: 22
Born: April 19, 1987
Birthplace: Nyagan, Soviet Union
Birth Name: Maria Yuryevna Sharapova

Notable Achievements

★ In 2008, *Forbes* Magazine named Sharapova the top-paid female athlete with an income of $26 million from tennis victories and endorsements.

★ Sharapova has won 19 career singles titles and 3 career doubles titles.

★ Sharapova was named ESPN Best Female Tennis Player in 2005 and 2007.

★ In 2007, Sharapova was named Goodwill Ambassador for the United Nations Development Programme.

Sharapova has won three Grand Slam titles—Wimbledon (2004), the US Open (2006), and the Australian Open (2008).

Super Stat

Singh won three major championships in his career—the Masters in 2000 and the PGA Championship in 1998 and 2004.

Super Stat

VIJAY SINGH

Age: 46
Born: February 22, 1963
Birthplace: Lautoka, Fiji
Birth Name: Vijay Singh

Notable Achievements

⭐ In 2004, Singh was ranked # 1 on the Official World Golf Ranking for 32 weeks.

⭐ Singh was the PGA Player of the Year in 2004, and also won the Vardon Trophy that year.

⭐ Singh was the leading PGA Tour money winner in 2003 and 2004.

⭐ In 2006, Singh was inducted into the World Golf Hall of Fame.

Smith holds the NFL's career rushing record with a total of 18,355 rushing yards.

Super Stat

EMMITT SMITH

Age: 40
Born: May 15, 1969
Birthplace: Pensacola, Florida
Birth Name: Emmitt James Smith III

Notable Achievements

⭐ Smith is the only player in the NFL to have 11 consecutive 1,000-yard rushing seasons. He also has the most rushing attempts in NFL history with 4,142.

⭐ In 1993, Smith became the only running back to win the Super Bowl, the Super Bowl MVP award, the NFL MVP award, and the NFL rushing crown in the same season.

⭐ Smith was selected to eight Pro Bowl games between 1990-1999.

⭐ With 164 career rushing touchdowns, Smith has more than any other running back.

Super Stat

ANNIKA SORENSTAM

Age: 39
Born: October 9, 1970
Birthplace: Bro, Sweden
Birth Name: Annika Sorenstam

Notable Achievements

⭐ Sorenstam has won more international victories than any other LPGA player with 90 wins. She has won 72 official LPGA tournaments.

⭐ Sorenstam has won 10 major LPGA tournaments, including three Kraft Nabisco championships (2001, 2002, 2005), three LPGA Championships (2003-2005), three US Women's Opens (1995, 1996, 2006), and one Women's British Open (2003).

⭐ Sorenstam holds the record for the most Player of the Year Awards with eight.

⭐ Sorenstam has won six Vare Trophies—the award given to the player with the lowest seasonal average.

White has won 14 X-Games medals for snowboarding and skateboarding since 2002—eight gold, four silver, and two bronze.

Super Stat

SHAUN WHITE

Age: 23
Born: September 3, 1986
Birthplace: Carlsbad, California
Birth Name: Shaun Roger White

Notable Achievements

⭐ White won an Olympic gold medal in Men's Halfpipe at the 2006 Torino Games.

⭐ In 2007, White won the overall gold medal in the TTR World Snowboard Tour.

⭐ White has won the halfpipe title at the US Open Snowboarding Championship for three consecutive years from 2006 to 2008.

⭐ White remains the only skateboarder to land the bodyvarial frontside 540. He was also the first to land a Cab 7 Melon Grab in vert skateboarding.

At the age of 12, Wie became the youngest person to make the cut for an LPGA event at the Kraft Nabisco Championship in 2003.

Super Stat

MICHELLE WIE

Age: 20
Born: October 11, 1989
Birthplace: Honolulu, Hawaii
Birth Name: Michelle Sung Wie

Notable Achievements

⭐ In 2004, Wie won the Laureus Newcomer of the Year Award.

⭐ At the Women's Amateur Public Links tournament in 2003, Wie became the youngest person ever to win a USGA adult event.

⭐ In 2004, Wie became the fourth female player ever to play in a PGA Tour.

⭐ In 2006, Wie became the first woman ever to qualify for the Asian Tour at the age of 16.

Williams won
Olympic gold medals
in doubles in Beijing
(2008) and Sydney
(2000).

**Super
Stat**

SERENA WILLIAMS

Age: 28
Born: September 26, 1981
Birthplace: Saginaw, Michigan
Birth Name: Serena Jameka Williams

Notable Achievements

⭐ Williams has won nine Grand Slam singles titles—three Australian Open victories (2003, 2005, 2007), one French Open victory (2002), two Wimbledon victories (2002, 2003), and three US Open victories (1999, 2002, 2008).

⭐ Williams is fifth in career prize money with her earnings totaling more than $20.2 million.

⭐ Williams has won seven Grand Slam doubles titles, including victories at the Australian Open twice, the French Open once, Wimbledon three times, and the US Open once.

⭐ Williams won the WTA Championship in 2001.

While playing at Wimbledon in 2008, Williams recorded the fastest serve in tournament history at 129 miles per hour.

Super Stat

VENUS WILLIAMS

Age: 29
Born: June 17, 1980
Birthplace: Lynwood, California
Birth Name: Venus Ebone Starr Williams

Notable Achievements

⭐ Williams has won 16 Grand Slam singles and doubles titles during her career—three at the Australian Open, three at the US Open, eight at Wimbledon, and two at the French Open.

⭐ Williams has won 37 singles titles and 11 doubles titles since turning pro in 1994.

⭐ Williams won two gold medals at the Olympic Games in Sydney in 2000—one in women's singles and one in women's doubles.

⭐ Williams has earned more than $20 million in career earnings.

Woods has 65 wins on the PGA Tour—the third most wins of all time.

Super Stat

TIGER WOODS

Age: 34
Born: December 30, 1975
Birthplace: Cypress, California
Birth Name: Eldrick Tont Woods

Notable Achievements

⭐ Woods has won 14 major championships—four Masters wins (1997, 2001, 2002, 2005), three US Open wins (2000, 2002, 2008), three Open Championships (2000, 2005, 2006), and four PGA Championships (1999, 2000, 2006, 2007).

⭐ Woods topped the *Sports Illustrated* highest-earning athlete list in 2007, bringing in almost $112 million—about $100 million in endorsements and almost $12 million in winnings.

⭐ Woods has been named PGA Player of the Year a record nine times.

⭐ Woods has won the Vardon Trophy a record seven times since turning pro in 1996.

More Star Stats

236

JJ Abrams

Age: 43
Born: June 27, 1966
Birthplace: New York, NY
Birth Name: Jeffrey Jacob Abrams

Notable Achievements

⭐ In 2006, Abrams won a Golden Globe for Best Television Series for *Lost*.

⭐ The first movie that Abrams directed was *Mission Impossible III*, which grossed $397.5 worldwide.

⭐ Abrams' production company, Bad Robot, has produced several successful television shows, including *Alias*, *Lost*, *What About Brian*, *Six Degrees*, and the new Fox hit *Fringe*.

⭐ Abrams was a writer for the blockbuster movie *Armageddon* in 1998, which grossed more than $554.6 million worldwide.

In 2005, Abrams won
two Emmy Awards for
the TV show *Lost*—
Outstanding Drama Series
and Outstanding Directing
for a Drama Series.

**Super
Stat**

In 2008, Banks won a Daytime Emmy Award for her talk show, *The Tyra Banks Show.*

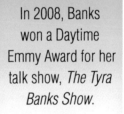

Super Stat

240

Tyra Banks

Age: 36
Born: December 4, 1973
Birthplace: Inglewood, California
Birth Name: Tyra Lynne Banks

Notable Achievements

⭐ Banks has been the host of the popular reality show—*America's Next Top Model*—since 2003.

⭐ Banks was the first African American woman to grace the covers of *GQ* and the *Sports Illustrated* Swim Suit Edition.

⭐ *Forbes* Magazine estimated that Banks earned $18 million in 2007 for her modeling and television work.

⭐ Banks has modeled for some of the most well-known fashion icons, including Chanel, Christian Dior, Dolce & Gabanna, Donna Karan, Oscar de la Renta, and Tommy Hilfiger.

Tyson Beckford

Age: 39
Born: December 19, 1970
Birthplace: Bronx, New York
Birth Name: Tyson Craig Beckford

Notable Achievements

⭐ Beckford has appeared in several music videos, including 50 Cent's "21 Questions," Britney Spears's "Toxic," and The Notorious B.I.G.'s "One More Chance."

⭐ Beckford is the host of Bravo's reality series *Make Me a Supermodel*.

⭐ In 1995, Beckford was named one of *People* Magazine's "50 Most Beautiful People of the World."

⭐ Beckford was named Man of the Year by music channel VH1 in 1995.

After a talent scout spotted him in a New York park, Beckford quickly became the face for Ralph Lauren's Polo clothing line.

Super Stat

243

Gisele Bündchen

Age: 29
Born: July 20, 1980
Birthplace: Rio Grande do Sol, Brazil
Birth Name: Gisele Caroline Nonnenmacher Bündchen

Notable Achievements

⭐ Since her debut in 1999, Bündchen has graced the covers of many fashion magazines, including *Vogue, ELLE, Allure, Harper's Bazaar, Vanity Fair, Marie Clare*, and *GQ*.

⭐ Bündchen has been the face of many top advertising campaigns, including Versace, Givenchy, Ralph Lauren, Victoria's Secret, Louis Vuitton, and Christian Dior.

⭐ Bündchen is one of just a few models to appear on three consecutive *Vogue* covers.

⭐ In 2000, Bündchen became only the fourth model in history to grace the cover of *Rolling Stone* Magazine.

Forbes Magazine ranks Bündchen as the highest-paid supermodel in the world, bringing in more than $35 million in 2008.

Super Stat

245

In June 2008, Burch won the CFDA award for Accessory Designer of the Year.

Super Stat

Tory Burch

Age: 41
Born: 1968
Birthplace: Valley Forge, Pennsylvania
Birth Name: Tory Burch

Notable Achievements

⭐ In November 2007, Burch won an award for Accessory Brand Launch of the Year by the Accessories Council of Excellence.

⭐ In 2005, the Fashion Group International awarded the Rising Star Award to Burch for best new Retail Concept.

⭐ Burch's clothing line brings in about $200 million in sales annually.

⭐ Burch did public relations for Vera Wang and Ralph Lauren before hitting it big after Oprah mentioned her accessories on the *Oprah Winfrey Show*.

Tom Colicchio

Age: 47
Born: August 15, 1962
Birthplace: Elizabeth, New Jersey
Birth Name: Thomas Patrick Colicchio

Notable Achievements

⭐ In 2000, Colicchio won the highly coveted James Beard's Best Chef New York Award.

⭐ In October 2002, Colicchio won *Bon Appetit* and the Food Network's Award for Chef of the Year in their American Food and Entertaining Awards.

⭐ Colicchio has several award-winning restaurants throughout the U.S., including Craft and Craftbar in New York, Craftsteak in Nevada, and Craft Dallas in Texas.

⭐ Colicchio's first cookbook, *Think Like a Chef* won a James Beard KitchenAid Cookbook Award in May 2001.

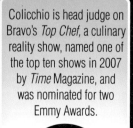

Colicchio is head judge on Bravo's *Top Chef*, a culinary reality show, named one of the top ten shows in 2007 by *Time* Magazine, and was nominated for two Emmy Awards.

Super Stat

Since opening his first store in 1996, Choo now has more than 60 locations worldwide.

Super Stat

Jimmy Choo

Awesome!

Age: 48
Born: 1961
Birthplace: Penang, Malaysia
Birth Name: Jimmy Choo Yeang Keat

Notable Achievements

⭐ The Jimmy Choo company is worth more than $364 million. Although Choo no longer designs shoes for his original company, he still churns out plenty of high-end footwear for celebrities and wealthy shoe shoppers with his exclusive Jimmy Choo Couture line.

⭐ In 2000, Choo was named Accessory Designer of the Year by the British Fashion Council.

⭐ In June 2003, Choo was awarded an OBE (Order of the British Empire) by the Queen of England because his London headquarters helped bring good fashion publicity to the city.

⭐ Choo's big break came when the UK's version of *Vogue* featured his shoes in a eight-page spread in 1988.

Since 1987, Chopra has written more than 50 books translated into 35 different languages. Several of these books have become *New York Times* bestsellers.

Super Stat

Deepak Chopra

Age: 63
Born: October 22, 1946
Birthplace: New Delhi, India
Birth Name: Deepak Chopra

Notable Achievements

⭐ Chopra is a fellow of the American College of Physicians, a member of the American Association of Clinical Endocrinologists, and Senior Scientist with The Gallup Organization.

⭐ Chopra created four music CDs and four videos between 1995 and 2004.

⭐ Chopra taught at Tufts University and Boston University. He also served as Chief of Staff at New England Memorial Hospital.

⭐ *Time* Magazine named Chopra one of the "Top 100 Heroes and Icons of the Century."

Ecko is a self-made billionaire, building an empire of companies in the fashion, publishing, art, gaming, and multimedia industries.

Super Stat

Marc Ecko

Age: 37
Born: 1972
Birthplace: East Brunswick, New Jersey
Birth Name: Marc Milecofsky

Notable Achievements

⭐ In 2007, Marc Ecko Enterprises reported international sales of approximately $1.5 billion.

⭐ Ecko received the first ever MTV Video Music Award in 2006 for "Best Video Game Soundtrack" with the release of "Marc Ecko's Getting Up: Contents Under Pressure."

⭐ Ecko has frequently been included in *Details* Magazine's "Most Powerful Men Under 40" list and *Stuff* Magazine's "Style Icons" list.

⭐ Ecko bought Barry Bond's historic 756th home run ball for $752,467 and donated it to the Baseball Hall of Fame.

Bobby Flay

Age: 45
Born: December 10, 1964
Birthplace: New York, NY
Birth Name: Robert William Flay

Notable Achievements

⭐ Flay has hosted seven shows for the Food Network. The five that are currently on the air include *FoodNation*, *Boy Meets Grill*, *BBQ with Bobby Flay*, *Throwdown! With Bobby Flay*, and *Grill It! With Bobby Flay*. He has been nominated for three Emmys and won one in 2005 for *Boy Meets Grill*.

⭐ Flay is an Iron Chef on the cooking show *Iron Chef America*.

⭐ In 2005, Flay won the James Beard Foundation's National Television Food Show Award for Bobby Flay Chef Mentor.

⭐ Flay graduated from the prestigious French Culinary Institute in New York City.

Flay is owner and executive chef of four hot restaurants—Bobby Flay Steak in New Jersey, Mesa Grill in Las Vegas, Mesa Grill in the Bahamas, and Mesa Grill and Bar Americain in New York.

Super Stat

Tommy Hilfiger

Age: 58
Born: March 24, 1951
Birthplace: Elmira, New York
Birth Name: Thomas Jacob Hilfiger

I'm a tommy girl! col

Notable Achievements

⭐ The Council of Fashion Designers of America named Hilfiger Menswear Designer of the Year in 1995.

⭐ In 1995, Hilfiger won the "From the Catwalk to the Sidewalk Award" at the first VH1 Fashion and Music Awards.

⭐ Hilfiger was named "Designer of the Year" by Parsons School of Design and by *GQ* Magazine.

⭐ Hilfiger starred in the TV reality series, *The Cut*, judging fashion contestants' designs in hopes of finding the next hot designer.

Hilfiger founded the Tommy Hilfiger Corporation in 1984, and within 20 years the fashion giant had 5,400 employees and revenues exceeding $1.8 billion.

Super Stat

Karan has created more than 20 signature fragrances for men and women, including Cashmere Mist, Chaos, DKNY Men, and DKNY Women.

Super Stat

Donna Karan

WOW OLD! /\/\/\/

Age: 61
Born: October 2, 1948
Birthplace: Forest Hills, New York
Birth Name: Donna Ivy Faske

Notable Achievements

⭐ The Council of Fashion Designers of America named Karan Menswear Designer of the Year 1992 and Womenswear Designer of the Year in 1990 and 1996. She later earned the Lifetime Achievement Award by the CFDA in 2004.

⭐ Karan won the Coty American Fashion Critics Award in 1977 and 1982. She was inducted into the Coty Hall of Fame in 1984.

⭐ There are 70 freestanding Donna Karan collection and DKNY stores worldwide.

⭐ Karan was the head of the Anne Klein design team from 1974 to 1985.

In 2008, *Forbes* Magazine ranked Klum as one of the highest paid models in the world with a salary of $14 million.

Super Stat

Heidi Klum

Pretty!

Age: 36
Born: June 1, 1973
Birthplace: Bergisch Gladbach, Germany
Birth Name: Heidi Klum

Notable Achievements

⭐ Klum has served as executive producer, host, and judge of the reality contest *Project Runway* since it first aired in 2004. In 2008, Klum won a Peabody Award for her work on the show—the first time a reality show earned the award. She has also received several Emmy nominations.

⭐ Klum has also had success as a designer, creating her own perfume, children's clothes, shoes, and jewelry lines.

⭐ Klum is the co-producer and host of *Germany's Next Topmodel*.

⭐ Klum has appeared in many advertising campaigns, including Liz Claiborne, McDonald's, Volkswagen, Jordache, and H & M.

Many of Kors's designs
have been worn by
stars on the big screen,
including Gwyneth Paltrow
(*Possessions*), Cate Blanchett
(*Bandits*), and Renee Russo
(*The Thomas Crown Affair*).

Super
Stat

266

Michael Kors

Age: 50
Born: August 9, 1959
Birthplace: Long Island, New York
Birth Name: Karl Anderson, Jr.

Notable Achievements

⭐ Kors's three clothing lines include the Michael Kors runway collection, MICHAEL Michael Kors and KORS Michael Kors, which launched between 2002 and 2004. In 2003, Kors won CFDA Award for Menswear Designer of the Year.

⭐ In 1999, Kors won the CFDA Award for Womenswear Designer of the Year.

⭐ Kors has written articles for *Harpers Bazaar*, and has interviewed Elizabeth Taylor and Jessica Simpson for the fashion magazine.

⭐ Kors has been a judge on *Project Runway*, the fashion reality series on Bravo.

Emeril Lagasse

Age: 50
Born: October 15, 1959
Birthplace: Fall River, Massachusetts
Birth Name: Emeril John Lagasse

Notable Achievements

⭐ Lagasse owns ten restaurants across the United States: in Atlanta, Orlando, Miami, Las Vegas and New Orleans. He has received many awards for his cooking, including the James Beard Foundation's "Best Southeast Regional Chef" in 1991 and "Restaurant of the Year" by *Esquire* Magazine.

⭐ Lagasse has hosted two programs for the Food Network— *The Essence of Emeril* and *Emeril Live*—and has received a total of eight Daytime Emmy nominations for the two shows.

⭐ Lagasse is a weekly food correspondent for ABC's *Good Morning America*.

⭐ Lagasse is the best-selling author of twelve cookbooks.

In 2007, Lagasse worked with NASA to create some recipes that would spice up the astronauts' meals in space.

Super Stat

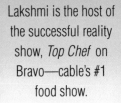

Lakshmi is the host of the successful reality show, *Top Chef* on Bravo—cable's #1 food show.

Super Stat

Padma Lakshmi

Age: 39
Born: September 1, 1970
Birthplace: Kerala, India
Birth Name: Padma Parvati Lakshmi

Notable Achievements

⭐ In 2006, Lakshmi appeared in *The Ten Commandments*, the second-highest rated television movie of the year.

⭐ Lakshmi is an ambassador for the United Nations Development Fund for Women.

⭐ Lakshmi has hosted the Food Network's *Padma's Passport*, as well as *Planet Food*.

⭐ Lakshmi's cookbook *Easy Exotic* was named Best First Book at the 1999 World Cookbook Awards.

Wolfgang Puck

Age: 60
Born: July 8, 1949
Birthplace: ankt Veit an der Glan, Austria
Birth Name: Wolfgang Johann Topfschnig

Notable Achievements

⭐ Puck's culinary empire includes Wolfgang Puck Fine Dining, which oversees the world-famous restaurant Spago; Wolfgang Puck Express, which has more than 80 locations throughout America; Wolfgang Puck Catering and Wolfgang Puck Worldwide, which include his own brands of soups, coffees, and pizzas.

⭐ Puck is the official caterer for the Governor's Ball following the Academy Awards.

⭐ Puck has won several prestigious awards, including the James Beard Award for "Outstanding Chef of the Year" and "Outstanding Restaurant of the Year" for Spago Beverly Hills.

⭐ Puck's Food Network program, *Wolfgang Puck,* won Daytime Emmy Awards for two consecutive years.

Puck has made several guest appearances on hit TV shows, including *Frasier*, *Las Vegas*, *American Idol*, and *Tales from the Crypt*.

Super Stat

273

Rachael Ray

KOOK!

Age: 41
Born: August 25, 1968
Birthplace: Glens Falls, New York
Birth Name: Rachael Domenica Ray

Notable Achievements

⭐ Ray has written 15 cookbooks, including the best-selling series *30-Minute Meals*.

⭐ Ray launched her own magazine, *Every Day with Rachael Ray* in 2006.

⭐ Ray has been a spokeswoman for several popular brands, including Dunkin' Donuts, Burger King, and Nabisco Crackers.

⭐ Ray has hosted five Food Network shows—*30 Minute Meals*, *Rachael Ray's Tasty Travels*, *$40 a Day*, *Inside Dish*, and *Rachael's Vacation*.

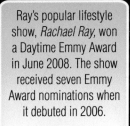

Ray's popular lifestyle show, *Rachael Ray,* won a Daytime Emmy Award in June 2008. The show received seven Emmy Award nominations when it debuted in 2006.

Super Stat

There are currently 25 Kate Spade boutiques around the world with sales of more than $125 million.

Super Stat

Kate Spade

need to see Fire-Stone

Age: 47
Born: 1962
Birthplace: Kansas City, Missouri
Birth Name: Katherine Noel Brosnahan

Notable Achievements

⭐ In 1996, Spade won Council of Fashion Designers of America's "America's New Fashion Talent in Accessories" award.

⭐ In 2004, *Bon Appetite, Elle Decor, and House Beautiful* all recognized Spade with awards for her home collection.

⭐ In 1998, Council of Fashion Designers of America named Spade the best accessory designer of the year.

⭐ Before becoming a designer, Spade was the senior fashion editor/head of accessories for *Mademoiselle* Magazine in 1991.

Vera Wang

U look like a guy

Age: 60
Born: June 27, 1949
Birthplace: New York, NY
Birth Name: Vera Wang

Notable Achievements

⭐ Wang opened her designer wedding gown salon in the ritzy Carlyle Hotel in 1990, and has since designed gowns for some of Hollywood's hottest stars, including Jennifer Lopez, Jessica Simpson, Victoria Beckham, Jennifer Garner, and Mariah Carey.

⭐ In 2005, the Council of Fashion Designers of America named Wang as Womenswear Designer of the Year.

⭐ Wang competed in the 1968 U.S. Figure Skating Championships and was featured in *Sports Illustrated*.

⭐ Wang has also designed some outfits for sports stars, including skating costumes for Nancy Kerrigan and Michelle Kwan, as well as the uniforms worn by the Philadelphia Eagles cheerleaders.

Wang joined *Vogue* at age 23, and became the youngest fashion editor in the history of the magazine.

Super Stat

Business & Money

Moguls ✦ Innovators ✦ Wealth ✦ Philanthropy

PAUL ALLEN

Age: 56
Born: January 21, 1953
Birthplace: Seattle, Washington
Birth Name: Paul Gardner Allen

Notable Achievements

⭐ Allen owns three professional sports teams—the Seattle Seahawks in the NFL, the Portland Trailblazers in the NBA, and the Seattle Sounder FC in MLS.

⭐ In 2008, Allen was named one of *Time Magazine's* 100 Most Influential People in the World.

⭐ Allen has won many awards, including the Regents' Distinguished Alumnus Award from Washington University, the Vanguard Award for Science and Technology from the National Cable & Telecommunications Association, and an honorary Doctor of Science degree from Watson School of Biological Sciences.

⭐ Through the Paul G. Allen Family Foundation, Allen awards about $30 million in grants each year.

As the co-founder of Microsoft, Allen is the 42nd richest man in the world with a net worth of more than $16 billion in 2008.

Super Stat

With a net worth of more than $22 billion, this heir to the L'Oreal cosmetic company fortune is the richest woman in the world.

Super Stat

LILIANE BETTENCOURT

Age: 87
Born: October 21, 1922
Birthplace: Paris, France
Birth Name: Liliane Bettencourt

Notable Achievements

⭐ Bettencourt is the principal shareholder of the L'Oreal company with 27.5% of its shares.

⭐ Bettencourt is the second-richest person in France, and the seventeenth-richest person in the world.

⭐ Bettencourt started the Bettencourt Schueller Foundation, which awards a prize to European researchers under the age of forty-five.

⭐ L'Oreal is the world's largest beauty company—consisting of Maybelline, Lancome, Redken, and many more companies—with annual sales topping $20 billion.

WARREN BUFFET

Age: 79
Born: August 30, 1930
Birthplace: Omaha, Nebraska
Birth Name: Warren Edward Buffet

Notable Achievements

⭐ In 2007, Buffet was named one of the "100 Most Influential People in the World" by *Time Magazine*.

⭐ In 2006, Buffet promised to give away much of his vast fortune, with more than three-quarters of it going to the Bill and Melinda Gates Foundation.

⭐ Known as the Oracle of Omaha, Buffet is considered one of the most successful investors in history.

⭐ As CEO of Berkshire Hathaway, Buffet earns a salary of just $100,000 a year.

Early in 2008, Buffet's net worth was estimated at $62 billion, which made him the richest person in the world. Later, his fortune was reduced to $50 billion.

Super Stat

MICHAEL DELL

Age: 44
Born: February 23, 1965
Birthplace: Houston, Texas
Birth Name: Michael Saul Dell

Dell laptops Rock!

Notable Achievements

⭐ As Dell, Inc.'s founder and CEO, Dell was worth more than $16 billion in 2008. The company is the most profitable PC manufacturer in the world with sales totaling more than $40 billion annually.

⭐ Dell has won many awards, including "Entrepreneur of the Year" from *Inc.* Magazine; "Man of the Year" from *PC* Magazine; "Top CEO in American Business" from *Worth* Magazine; and "CEO of the Year" from *Financial World* and *Industry Week* magazines.

⭐ In 2006, the Michael and Susan Dell Foundation awarded a $50 million grant to the University of Texas at Austin.

⭐ In 2000, Dell topped *Fortune* Magazine's list of the richest self-made Americans under 40.

In 1992 at the age of 27, Dell was the youngest CEO of a Fortune 500 company.

Super Stat

As the co-founder and CEO of Oracle Corporation, Ellison is the fourteenth-richest person in the world with a net worth of $25 billion in 2008.

Super Stat

LAWRENCE ELLISON

Age: 65
Born: August 17, 1944
Birthplace: New York, New York
Birth Name: Lawrence Joseph Ellison

Notable Achievements

⭐ Oracle's database software is the most widely used in the world, supporting about 95% of all Fortune 100 companies.

⭐ In 1997, Ellison spent $250 million to established the Ellison Medical Foundation to fund studies into aging and infectious diseases.

⭐ Ellison is a competitive sailor and has competed in the America's Cup for several years.

⭐ Ellison owns the fifth-largest yacht in the world—*the Rising Sun*—measuring 452 feet long. He also owns a fighter jet and a McLaren F1 sports car.

The Bill and Melinda Gates Foundation is one of the largest charitable foundations in the world and has given more than $16 billion since it was formed in 2000.

Super Stat

BILL GATES

Age: 54
Born: October 28, 1955
Birthplace: Seattle, Washington
Birth Name: William Henry Gates III

Notable Achievements

⭐ As of September 2008, Gates was the richest person in America, with a net worth of $61 billion. He ranked in the top spot of the *Forbes* list from 1993 to 2008.

⭐ Gates co-founded Microsoft with Paul Allen at the age of 20, and today the company is worth more than $51 billion.

⭐ *Time Magazine* named Gates one of the "100 People Who Most Influenced the 20th Century," and also named him one of the "Most Influential People" of 2004, 2005, and 2006.

⭐ Gates scored 1590 out of 1600 on his SATs and was accepted at Harvard University in 1973.

NICOLAS HAYEK

Age: 81
Born: February 19, 1928
Birthplace: Beirut, Lebanon
Birth Name: Nicolas George Hayek

Notable Achievements

⭐ The Swatch Group is the top manufacturer of finished watches in the world.

⭐ Hayek helped to create the tiny Smart Car for Mercedes Benz.

⭐ Several Swatch Group companies serve as official timekeepers at international sports events, including the Olympic Games.

⭐ In 1996, Hayek was awarded *doctor honoris causa* of Law and Economics of the University if Neuchatel in Switzerland.

ur eyebrows don't wanna meet Myra! but tht would help tht rest of us!

SWAT

As co-founder and chairman of the board of directors of the Swatch Group, Hayek is worth more than $3.2 billion.

Super Stat

STEVE JOBS

Age: 54
Born: February 24, 1955
Birthplace: San Francisco, California
Birth Name: Steven Paul Jobs

Notable Achievements

⭐ Jobs—the co-founder, CEO, and Chairman of Apple, Inc.—is worth more than $5 billion. The self-made billionaire also created the iPhone, which made $330 million during its first weekend of sales in 2008.

⭐ As the co-founder of Pixar Animation Studios, Jobs was behind several blockbuster movies, including *Toy Story, Monsters, Inc., Finding Nemo*, and *Cars*.

⭐ In 1985, Jobs was awarded the National Medal of Technology from President Ronald Reagan.

⭐ Jobs is Walt Disney Company's largest individual shareholder and is part of the company's board of directors.

In 2007, Jobs was listed as *Fortune* Magazine's Most Powerful Businessman.

Super Stat

Johnson oversees the Personal and Workplace Investing division of Fidelity—a company that has $1.5 trillion in managed assets.

Super Stat

ABIGAIL JOHNSON

Age: 48
Born: December 19, 1961
Birthplace: Boston, Massachusetts
Birth Name: Abigail Pierrepont Johnson

Notable Achievements

⭐ Johnson runs part of Fidelity Investments—America's largest investment company—and has a net worth of $15 billion. She is the third-richest American woman and the forty-third richest person in the world.

⭐ Johnson earned her MBA from Harvard University.

⭐ Johnson ran her first fund in 1993 and took over the mutual fund division in 2001.

⭐ Johnson was included in CNN's Top 50 Most Powerful Women in 2007.

JUDY McGRATH

Age: 57
Born: July 15, 1952
Birthplace: Scranton, Pennsylvania
Birth Name: Judith Ann McGrath

Notable Achievements

⭐ McGrath's MTV Network channels reach 400 million viewers in 164 countries and bring in nearly $3 billion in profits annually.

⭐ The MTV Network also has about 300 websites, including Atomfilms, Shockwave, and Neopets.

⭐ McGrath was on board when MTV's *The Real World* launched, paving the way for reality television.

⭐ McGrath's VH1 Save the Music Foundation has given away $34 million in new musical instruments to more than 1,400 public schools.

McGrath is the Chairman and CEO of MTV Networks and oversees MTV, VH-1, Comedy Central, and Nickelodeon.

Super Stat

Trump owns the largest piece of land in New York City—a 100-acre property along the Hudson River which will be become a $5 billion project known as Trump Place.

Super Stat

DONALD TRUMP

Age: 63
Born: June 14, 1946
Birthplace: New York, New York
Birth Name: Donald John Trump

Notable Achievements

⭐ Trump is CEO of the real estate development company Trump Organization, operating many lush properties including Trump World Tower and Trump Tower in New York, and 555 California Street in San Francisco. Together, the value of Trump's properties totals more than $3 billion.

⭐ Trump is paid by developers to license and promote their properties, which has brought in $562 million.

⭐ Trump is also the founder of Trump Entertainment Resorts, including Trump Plaza, Trump Taj Mahal, and Trump Marina.

⭐ Trump is the host and executive producer of the successful NBC reality show, *The Apprentice.*

Oprah's Angel Network began in 1998 and has since raised more than $51 million for charitable programs.

Super Stat

OPRAH WINFREY

Age: 55
Born: January 29, 1954
Birthplace: Kosciusko, Mississippi
Birth Name: Oprah Gail Winfrey

Notable Achievements

⭐ Oprah is the most powerful person in Hollywood with a net worth of $2.7 billion. The media mogul earns $385 million a year. Oprah has topped *Forbes* Most Powerful Celebrity list in 2005, 2007, and 2008.

⭐ Oprah has won more than 40 Daytime Emmy Awards since the *Oprah Winfrey Show* began in 1986. More than 49 million viewers tune in each week.

⭐ Oprah also has her own radio channel on XM Satellite Radio, and two magazines—*O, The Oprah Magazine* and *O At Home*.

⭐ Oprah.com averages more than 70 million page views and more than six million users per month.

JERRY YANG

Age: 41
Born: November 6, 1968
Birthplace: Taipei, Taiwan
Birth Name: Jerry Yang

Notable Achievements

⭐ Yang, CEO of Yahoo!, has a net worth of $2.3 billion. The self-made billionaire met David Filo at Stanford University and co-founded Yahoo! in 1995. The company went public two years later.

⭐ Yahoo! now has 12,000 employees and more than 500 million unique visitors.

⭐ Yang serves as a member of the Board of Trustees of Stanford University.

⭐ Yang pledged $75 million to Stanford University to construct an environmental studies building.

Yang's stake in Yahoo! is worth about $1.4 billion. However, he's paid just $1 a year.

Super Stat

MARK ZUCKERBERG

Age: 24
Born: May 14, 1984
Birthplace: White Plains, New York
Birth Name: Mark Elliott Zuckerberg

Notable Achievements

- The Harvard dropout created Facebook in 2004 and it now boasts 66 million users and $150 million in annual sales.

- Zuckerberg is CEO of Facebook and has a 30% stake in the company.

- Microsoft bought 1.6% of Facebook in 2007 for $240 million.

- In 2008, *Forbes* Magazine declared that Zuckerberg is one of the youngest billionaires in history.

Zuckerberg—the genius behind the online social site Facebook—is worth $1.5 billion.

Super Stat

Index

Index

Index